Adding Realism to Your Model Railway

Adding Realism to Your Model Railway

Michael Andress

Patrick Stephens

First published in 1988

British Library Cataloguing in Publication Data

Andress, Michael
    Adding realism to your model railway.
    1. Railroad — Models
    I. Title
    625.1'9   TF197

    ISBN 0-85059-845-1

Cover illustrations
Front *A realistic view on 'Wigleton', an EM gauge layout built by Tony Hills. The figures with the horse and cart add life and interest to the scene* (Len Weal).
Back *A scene showing just how interesting and attractive a wintry snow and ice setting can be for a model railway. This is part of Roger Desoutter's HO scale Swiss prototype 'Wintertal'* (Len Weal)

Patrick Stephens Limited is part of the Thorsons Publishing Group, Wellingborough, Northamptonshire, NN8 2RQ, England.

Printed in Great Britain by Woolnough Bookbinding Limited, Irthlingborough, Northamptonshire

10 9 8 7 6 5 4 3 2 1

Contents

Introduction

My interest in railway modelling goes back a good many years and as I am something of a collector, some would say hoarder, I have over this time acquired a fairly sizeable library of magazines on the subject. A browse through these back issues of model railway journals is always enjoyable and relaxing, and it can also be rewarding as I often rediscover information and ideas previously read but since forgotten, or which have been missed altogether the first time around. Not infrequently, I come across construction methods or other hints and tips which I ignored at the time of publication as they did not appear relevant to my modelling then but which are now helpful for current projects.

Looking through old and recent issues in this way can also provide an interesting and instructive overall perspective of just how the hobby has developed over the period they cover. On a recent search through my collection of back issues of model railway magazines for some specific information I required, I soon, and not too reluctantly, became side-tracked into a general browse. I was interested to notice just how much improvement there has been

generally in the standards of realism and attractiveness of layouts over the years. There are, of course, some exceptions to this generalization, some outstanding layouts which were ahead of their time in approach and execution. I was inspired in my early railway modelling days, as I am sure many others were, by layouts such as John Ahern's 'Madder Valley Railway', John Allen's 'Gorre & Daphetid Railroad' and P.D. Hancock's narrow gauge 'Craig & Mertonford Railway'. These fine examples of skilful and imaginative modelling led the way in the development of realism and one can still learn from studying pictures of them. Since then, there have been other excellent layouts which have further advanced the progress toward greater realism.

Even apart from these outstanding layouts, there has been a considerable overall improvement in standards of realism and from curiosity I looked to see how this has been achieved. Clearly the improvement is partly due to the increased range, quality and standards of accuracy and detailing of the commercially available products. These include such diverse items as ready-to-run and kit locomotives and rolling-stock, structure kits, accessories, detailing parts, scenic texture materials and many others. The standard of modelling work by the enthusiast has also improved significantly. Structure models, for example, are more accurate with greater detailing. This does not necessarily mean that the modeller is now more skilful or that the hobby is more difficult for the beginner to participate in. I think that it is more a question of a higher standard of finish being usual, so that modellers expect to put more time and effort into constructing models to reach this standard. There have also been changes in approach and emphasis which have been very significant, in particular the concept of modelling a landscape of which the railway is only part rather than modelling a railway almost in isolation.

From this point I went on to consider how a layout can be made more realistic and interesting and the idea of this book was born. Most modellers are keen to make their layouts more realistic, and in this book I want to look at what we mean by realism, why we might want to achieve it, and how we may do so. For the most part I am not seeking to add realism by improvement in the actual technical modelling skill of the enthusiast. This automatically comes with practice and experience, and by far the best way to develop one's ability in this respect is to do lots of modelling. I am hoping rather to make more effective use of skills already possessed, by choosing the right approach to create overall realism. Nor do I want to claim that the ideas presented here will automatically make for an outstanding layout. I do hope, however, that they may help you to make your layout that little bit more realistic, interesting and satisfying.

The book is not intended to be a com-

prehensive modelling guide. Instead, I want to look at various specific model railway features with some ideas and information on how their realism may be improved and enhanced to the benefit of the layout as a whole. I have chosen topics where I feel, for various reasons, that particular benefit in increased realism can be achieved for the modelling work required. In other words, I have tried to select aspects of the layout where maximum effect will result from the effort involved. This is all to the good whenever possible, not only because most of us are busy and have only limited time for modelling, but also because being able to see an improvement fairly quickly encourages further effort and yet more benefit in terms of realism.

Because the scenic setting, taken in its broadest sense to include everything except the trains themselves, is so important in creating overall realism, most of the book is devoted to its various aspects. However, although the standards of accuracy and detail of the locomotives and rolling-stock now on the market are generally good, some significant improvements can still be fairly readily made. The appearance of the ready-to-run diesel locomotive models benefits from the addition of extra detailing, particularly at the front and rear ends, and I am grateful to Chris Ellis for his contribution on this subject. Chris is the editor of *Scale Model Trains* magazine and he has considerable experience of detailing and improving commercial locomotive models, including almost all of the currently available diesels. The realism of locomotives and rolling-stock is also greatly enhanced by the application of appropriate weathering, and that is an important topic covered in this book.

The photography of models, including railway models, is now a popular pastime. With the inclusion of a section on model railway photography in this book you may feel that I am digressing from my stated theme of adding realism to merely portraying it. However, the very features which make for good pictures also add to the realism and effectiveness of a layout. So the development of a 'photographer's eye' for a good picture can only enhance your ability to design and build realistic scenes on your layout.

Moreover, though the theme of this book is adding realism, it is also important for the layout to be interesting; there is little to be gained from a very realistic model which for one reason or another is boring to view or operate. The selection of a suitable prototype is essential, and choosing one which is a little out of the ordinary can help to make your layout different and interesting. One option which has much to recommend it is to model a foreign railway. Giles Barnabe decided to model the Majorcan Railway as a change from a British prototype and I am grateful to him for the account of his experiences.

I would like to thank all those modellers who have kindly allowed me to use photographs of their models to illustrate various points in this book. I am particularly grateful to Malcolm Carlsson, Mike Gill, Derek Purkis, Dave Rowe and Len Weal, and to John Brewer and David Lloyd of *Railway Modeller* and *Continental Modeller* magazines.

Affweigh station on Ron Boreham's N scale Southern Railway branch set in the 1960s. The addition of a dummy outside third rail has contributed to the atmosphere of the scene and helped to provide a realistic setting for the 2-car electric multiple unit.

CHAPTER 1
Realism: What? Why? How?

It is perhaps logical to consider first of all just what we are trying to achieve and what we mean by 'realism' in the context of railway modelling. It might not unreasonably be thought that if we can copy part of the prototype railway exactly to scale then we would have a realistic model. In fact, though an accurate model dimensionally, this would probably not be very interesting or satisfying, particularly as a very large area would be required to model much of the real railway. In the creation of realism in railway modelling, we require an artist's representation rather than a precise scaled down reproduction. We are aiming to give the impression and atmosphere of the subject, to reproduce the features which give it appeal and character, while omitting irrelevant or undesirable features. The overall impression is more important than the precise accuracy of the component parts.

Realism is not an easy concept to

Attractive and realistically modelled structures and scenery on the Milton Model Railway Group 'Woolbridge' layout provide a setting which enhances the appearance of the locomotives and rolling-stock. This 7mm fine scale layout is based on the London & South Western Railway.

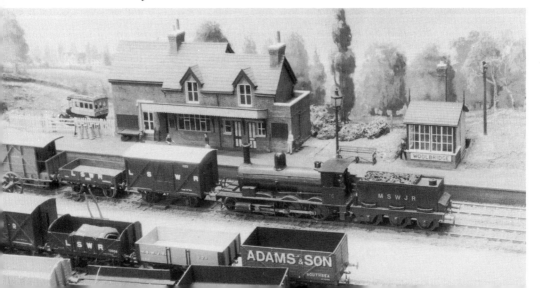

The modern concept of modelling the railway as part of the landscape as a whole has added greatly to the realism of layouts. This approach is seen at its best on the Model Railway Club's 2mm scale Chiltern Green layout (Len Weal).

define, but my dictionary gives the following definition which seems reasonably apt, even though I am sure it was not penned with railway modelling in mind: 'Realism: fidelity of representation, truth to nature, insistence upon detail'.

We may also ask ourselves if greater realism is worth the extra effort. Most modellers will be keen to make their layouts as realistic as they can, and such models will be generally more attractive, interesting and satisfying. As one does more modelling, one's skill and experience increase and develop and the models constructed become more

Left *The scenery and structures not only make a model railway more interesting to look at but also help to show the viewer where the layout is set. Even the casual onlooker will recognise the desert landscape and the buildings of the American West, more specifically Arizona, on the Dabble Creek & Greenfield Railroad, an N scale layout built by Bill Fellows.*

Below *The scenic setting is also important in establishing the period represented on the model. This evocative Victorian scene, circa 1860, was created in 3.5mm scale (HO) by Malcolm Carlsson. The carriage and the figures in period costume give the atmosphere of the time* (Malcolm Carlsson).

The atmosphere of a country branch of the Great Western Railway has been successfully captured in this scene of a tree-lined lane crossing a single track line on a Ratio exhibition module.

realistic; this continuing improvement in standard is also very gratifying. For most of us, much of the appeal of the hobby is in the creation of a replica in miniature of a prototype scene which we find attractive and interesting, and the more realistic the model the more pleasing and enjoyable the hobby will be. Much of the fun comes from the actual construction work, so most modellers will not mind putting extra effort into building if the results are better.

Having said that, it is important to remember that this is a hobby, for relaxation and enjoyment and a chance to opt out of the 'rat race' at least for a few hours at a time. If your model railway gives you pleasure and enjoyment in its construction and operation then it is a success regardless of its realism or other-

wise. Don't feel that you have to 'compete' with others, or that your layout must be super-detailed, or that you must build to some specific standards of accuracy or to fine scale standards. Nor should you be concerned that you are not skilful enough to build a realistic model railway. As with most activities, there is no substitute for actual practice and experience in improving skill and ability. You will soon find that you are able to carry out most modelling work competently enough to create an attractive layout. As we shall see, reasonable modelling ability with the right approach is more important than great technical skill in construction.

How then are we to go about making our layouts more realistic? I have already implied that we are aiming for overall realism, with the building of a miniature scene which recreates for us the atmosphere and features of the prototype which stimulated us to want to model it in the first place. Precise scale modelling down to every last rivet can produce very impressive models, but is not essential for overall realism. Generally, the standard of accuracy and detail of commercially produced locomotives and rolling stock is quite adequate for a realistic appearance, though improvements can be made with advantage in some areas. For example, extra detail-

ing, particularly to the ends, enhances the appearence of the commercially available ready-to-run diesel locomotive models and Chris Ellis has described how to do this in a later section of this book.

It is in the scenic setting that there is the greatest scope for improving realism and giving your layout individuality. I use the term 'scenic setting' in its broad sense to include structures, details, figures and so on, as well as the actual scenic landscape. It is in the modelling of the setting particularly that simple

Town scenery can also form an effective setting for a model railway. In this scene on Robert Tivendale's Ashley Bridge 00 scale layout, low-relief shops lining a road running above and behind the station complete the scene very realistically (Len Weal).

Excellent landscape modelling has created a feeling of spaciousness and realism on the Model Railway Club's 2mm scale Chiltern Green layout (Len Weal).

dimensional accuracy of reproduction is quite inappropriate. Here the selective artistic approach is important to give the right impression, and colour and texture are very important. The modeller should not be discouraged by the idea that some special artistic ability or training is required. Most important are observation of the real thing and the selection of key features in the scene which will give the right atmosphere and character.

After considering some of the general principles involved, I want to look at various aspects of the scenic setting in which a little extra work and attention to detail will be well rewarded in enhanced realism and interest.

CHAPTER 2
Observation

Observation of the real thing is essential. We would not attempt to model a goods wagon, for example, without looking carefully at it, or referring to photographs and plans to guide us in its construction, yet when it comes to modelling the scenic setting many modellers seem to feel that this reference to the prototype is unnecessary. They just make something up, probably following rather stereotyped ideas based perhaps on other model railway layouts they have seen. Much can be learned from a study of good layouts in seeing how problems have been tackled and

overcome, but it is not a substitute for observing the real locality on which you want to base your layout's scenery.

If we are hoping to create a realistic model we must know what the real thing looks like so that we know exactly what appearance we are trying to reproduce. We need to look at the broader aspects which give the general character of the area — the contours of the land, whether flat, hilly, undulating or mountainous, whether farmland, marsh, moorland or desert, the types of trees and other vegetation, the colours of the foliage, the type of architecture and building

Above *A delightful period street scene modelled in 4mm scale also by Mike Gill. The buildings were scratch-built and are closely based on real structures. The sloping street adds to the interest and authenticity of the model* (Mike Gill).

Below left *Careful observation of the real thing and skilful modelling has enabled Mike Gill to create this very realistic 4mm scale model of a rather dilapidated thatched cottage* (Mike Gill).

Below *General views of your chosen prototype are useful in showing the grouping of structures, the type of landscape and how the two blend. This is a view of the Boston Lodge locomotive works on the Festiniog Railway. Note also the smaller details visible in the picture such as the notice-board and the check rail on the sharply curved line in the foreground.*

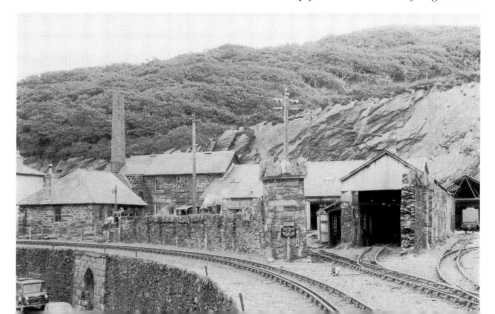

Left *A more detailed view taken near the one on the previous page shows the stone construction of the wall and the stone slab steps leading down to the road. Note also the derelict shelter at the top of the steps.*

Right *Luton Hoo station and signal cabin on the Model Railway Club's 2mm scale Chiltern Green layout. The many accurately modelled small details add greatly to the realism of the scene* (Len Weal).

Below *This view of Leicester Station shows a typical city skyline in the background and would be a useful guide for modelling such a scene.*

materials and so on. We must get the feel of the area, a lasting impression which will help us when modelling it and which will also make sure that whatever we include in our landscape will be in keeping with the real scene. It is very easy to spoil the effect of an otherwise well-modelled scene by including a few features or details which are inappropriate. Even though it may not be evident exactly what is wrong, the atmosphere will be spoilt and instead of giving the character and feel of a specific area recognizable to anyone who knows the prototype, the scene will become a nondescript representation of nowhere in particular. By being really familiar with the real thing, we can avoid such errors as we will realize that some features are not right for the area we are modelling.

It is not necessary to be a geologist, geographer or botanist so long as we can observe and research well. We don't need to know how the landscape came to look as it does, providing we are familiar with its present appearance. Small details are important because they help to add character to a scene. They are often overlooked because we tend to take them for granted, so it is useful to note them for future reference.

A superbly modelled industrial scene in 4mm scale by Dave Rowe. The model is based on the Leighton Buzzard sand quarries and the structures are authentic, beautifully detailed and realistically weathered. The canal contains real water (Peco).

CHAPTER 3
Collecting ideas and information

I have already stressed the importance of familiarity with the area on which you want to base your model and the type of scenery you wish to represent. Ideally you should visit the locale to see it at first hand, though it is possible, but more difficult, to build a successful layout based only on information obtained from other sources such as books, postcards, magazine articles, brochures and so on. Obviously it is most convenient to model the area in which you live or one which is within easy reach. You can then obtain all the general information you require without difficulty and you can also easily go and check or recheck on any specific points which arise in planning or construction as and when you need to.

However, with a little more effort and pre-planning, a more distant locale can be successfully modelled. Mike and David Polglaze, for example, have built a large HO scale Swiss standard gauge prototype layout in their loft and a smaller HO scale Swiss metre gauge portable layout which has been shown at a number of exhibitions. The very realistic feel and atmosphere of Swiss railways is the result of careful research in books and magazines and several holiday visits to the country centred on the areas being

modelled. On these trips they made copious notes and sketches of all relevant aspects of the railways, the lineside details and the scenic setting generally, supplemented by numerous photographs, mainly in colour. All the information was carefully kept in a series of notebooks and photograph albums, providing a detailed source of reference during the planning and construction of the layouts.

This visiting, exploring and documenting, whether close to home, further afield in Britain or far away overseas, can be very enjoyable and interesting in itself and can add another dimension to an already very satisfying hobby. Because you have a definite purpose, the gathering of ideas and information for the development of your model railway layout, you will find that you notice more and have a greater interest in and appreciation of your surroundings. There is also great pleasure and a sense of achievement when you find just the scene, structure or other feature you want to model to really enhance part of your layout. You will also come across features which, though typical enough to be included appropriately on your model railway, are a little out of the

Above *Collect pictures of the scenery for the area in which you plan to set your layout. This view of a light railway bridge would be a useful guide when modelling a small river and its grassy banks.*

Below *Even when, as here, the tracks have been lifted after closure of the line, the track-bed often remains with the route still clearly visible, and sometimes bridges and other features are left intact.*

ordinary and which will give your layout individuality as well as authenticity.

While there is much to be gained by just wandering and observing, and absorbing the feel of the place, it is also important to make a permanent record. Later, when you are planning and building your layout, you will then have all the information you require easily to hand. Always carry a pen or pencil, a notebook and, if possible, a camera with you on these trips. Make notes covering anything and everything you feel will be relevant. If you are one of those talented people who can sketch well, this will be very valuable in collecting information and in developing ideas for possible scenes on the layout. Even if your drawing ability, like mine, leaves much to be desired, you can still make rough drawings which will be adequate as a record, especially if you keep them fairly simple and if you note down enough dimensions, where relevant, from which to make a reasonably accurate model. Remember that is is often clearer to interpret later if you make several simple sketches showing various aspects of, for example, a building, than if you try to include too much information on one picture.

Personally, I find photography the most convenient method and I carry my camera with me whenever I think I may be going to places where I may find structures or scenery of interest. If you have one of the small automatic 35mm cameras which are now very popular, you can carry it quite easily in a pocket and it will always be ready to record any scenes you come across; this is ideal, as I often seem to find the most interesting features when my camera has been left at home! When I am out on a photographic trip of this sort, I tend to take too many

rather than too few pictures. It is worth taking plenty of pictures when the opportunity arises even if the information may not appear to be of immediate use, as it may avoid the need for a further trip to obtain more information later. It is useful to build up as comprehensive a photographic collection as you can of the scenery and structures which will form the setting, as well as, of course, of the railway itself. You will then find that not only is the information readily available when you need it for modelling, but also that a look through your files will often give you ideas and inspiration for other features and projects for the layout that you had not perhaps previously considered.

As black and white film is relatively inexpensive, particularly if you load your own 35mm cassettes using the tins of film sold for bulk loading, it is worth taking plenty of pictures. For structures, for example, straight-on views of front, sides and back are useful for modelling purposes, and if you can include a person of known height in the pictures this will enable you to estimate the dimensions sufficiently well to draw up plans and build a model. Photographs are also very good for collecting information on small details which you can model, even if the structure as a whole is unsuitable for your purposes. Modelling such features accurately will add authenticity and realism to your model buildings. Industrial structures in particular often have a great deal in the way of pipes, ducts, tanks, valves, ventilators, extractors and so on visible on the exterior, and adding such features to your models will make them more interesting.

There is no need to model any building exactly as you find it unless you

This general view of a waterside industrial area is an example of a record picture from my files. Note the typical structures which could be modelled very effectively in low relief at the rear of a layout, and the many small details suitable for inclusion on a model scene.

wish to. Often alterations will make it more suitable for the situation it will occupy on your layout, while combining features from several different prototypes may result in the most appropriate building for the scene you are modelling.

Photography can be used in the same way to record features of the scenery. The shape of a rocky outcrop, the appearance of the bank of a stream, the way trees are grouped, details of hedges and fences and so on. Again you will probably find that you will want to build up a scene for your layout from a combination of different features rather than by reproducing a single scene. The camera is also ideal for recording the many small details which are otherwise often difficult to recall but which must be right if the scene is to look realistic.

Though the film is more expensive, it is best to take at least some colour pictures if possible. Obviously colour is very important on the layout, and even though colour film reproduction is not always accurate it will be a very useful guide to the colouring and painting of scenery and structures. The pictures are also a helpful guide for weathering purposes. If you have two cameras, one could be used for black and white and

This photograph of a Cornish fishing village with its houses built up the hillside shows how varying levels make the scene more interesting. Duplicating this in model form is not only attractive but also saves space on the layout.

the other for colour; if you and a friend work together and each have a camera, it would be worthwhile using them in this way. If you cannot take colour pictures, it is important to keep a written note of the colours in your notebook; at least then you will have some idea of what the colours were when you come to model from your black and white photographs and sketches.

If you do take a considerable number of pictures, it is desirable to have some form of filing system which will permit convenient storage and retrieval of your negatives. I use mainly 35mm film and I store the negatives in Paterson and

Photo Science negative files which are loose-leaf folders holding separate sheets each of which will take a 36 exposure 35mm film cut into strips of six pictures. Before filing the negatives, I contact print each film on to a sheet of 10 in by 8 in enlarging paper in a Paterson contact printer. The contact sheet for each film is then filed with the loose-leaf holding the film. This makes it easier to locate the negative for a particular picture, but ideally the negatives should also be cross-indexed according to subject. A simple method is to give each sheet and each negative on that sheet a number; for example, 12/4 would be the 4th negative on sheet 12. File cards are then made up for different subjects, for example signal boxes, and are filed alphabetically. The relevant negative numbers are then listed on the cards together with any further brief identifying notes that you wish to include. Colour pictures can be filed away using a similar system of cards or can be mounted into albums for reference or browsing through to get the feel of the area pictured.

If you cannot visit the locality you wish to model, it is still possible to obtain a good deal of data but it may require rather more searching to acquire, particularly if you have chosen a somewhat obscure or exotic place. Your local public library may be able to help with books illustrating the area, preferably in colour. Look also for books showing buildings, street scenes and other features typical of the locality. You may also be able to find information on the railways and related structures, often with some more general views showing the scenery and terrain, in railway and model railway books and magazines.

Whatever approach you use, try to give yourself time to absorb the information and to get the feel of the locale before rushing too quickly into modelling it. The preliminary research can be a very enjoyable part of the hobby and can make your travel, holidays and reading even more interesting than they would be without this added goal.

Different areas and different railway companies have characteristic railway architecture both in style and in the materials employed in construction. It is important to build up a collection of pictures as a record to guide you in choosing appropriate structures for your layout. This photograph of a goods shed at Chester-le-Street in County Durham is typical of the sort of record picture it is useful to have on file. If necessary, the dimensions can be calculated approximately by using the track gauge as a guide.

A scene on the H0 scale metre gauge 'Die Bernhardinbahn' layout built by David and Mike Polglaze. The model is based on part of the Swiss Rhaetian Railway which was planned but never built and much information has been collected on holiday visits to Switzerland to enable a realistic layout to be constructed.

If you choose to model an exotic and distant prototype, you will need to make the most of any visit to build up a file of information and photographs, such as this picture of a simple wooden shelter at a small halt on a line in Thailand.

CHAPTER 4
Planning

Some layouts start simply, perhaps as a basic oval from a train set, and are then extended in a rather random fashion as space and finances permit. Sometimes a track plan may be found in a book or magazine which appears to offer good operational prospects. Alternatively, perhaps a layout is designed so as to fit as much track as possible into the space available; scenery is then added as an afterthought to fill the space between the tracks. Not surprisingly, these approaches do not usually give a very realistic result.

Planning is essential for a realistic model railway and there are various aspects to be considered. We should begin with a basic theme or concept providing a reason for the existence of the line. Real railways are constructed for a definite purpose; this may be to move slate from quarries in the hills down to a port for shipment, or to carry raw materials from dock to factory, or to transport passengers, and so on. Often there are combinations with many dif-

Above and below *David Pennington's fine model of Stanmore station, London & North Western Railway, in the period around 1908 has been based on study of numerous photographs of the prototype collected over a period of years. The layout is 4mm scale, EM gauge. The attractive and interesting prototype buildings have been beautifully modelled from scratch.*

Below left *Colin Hayward's model of Lee-on-the-Solent is a fine example of a replica of a specific prototype and captures the atmosphere of this Victorian/Edwardian seaside resort particularly well. The superb scratch-built structures are accurate models of the original buildings.*

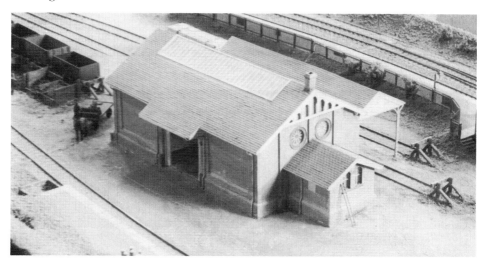

ferent items being carried from place to place. Thus, if a model railway is to be realistic it must also appear to be providing such a service.

If we have chosen to model a specific prototype, the history, geography and purpose of the line is already established and we have our basic concept. If, however, we are not modelling a real railway location we do need to give some thought to the purpose and background of our line if we hope to achieve realism. Such a line may be completely imaginary, both railway and setting — the 'freelance' railway layout. These were popular at one time, with the modeller creating not only the location — a fictitious island off the British coast was sometimes chosen — but also the

locomotive and rolling-stock designs and the railway architecture for their imaginary railway companies. Don't be misled into thinking that this was an easy alternative to the research required for a model based on a specific prototype. For a convincing freelance mode!, considerable planning is needed and the modeller must develop a clear idea of the geography, history and purpose of his line as well as decide on many other aspects such as size and type of locomotive, style and materials employed in building construction and so on. This can be much more difficult than merely following the practice of a real railway and it must be carried out convincingly if the result is to be realistic. Nowadays, freelance model

Mike Walshaw's 00 scale 'Westport' layout is an example of a 'might have been' line. It represents a Southern Railway branch line in the early to mid-1950s serving an imaginary town on the Dorset coast between Swanage and Weymouth. The model follows Southern Railway practice and its timetable is based on the actual timetable employed for the Swanage branch.

railways are rare except for narrow gauge layouts.

More popular now are lines which though not modelled on a specific prototype location are based on actual railways. This approach can take various forms. One is to build a line based, for example, on the GWR but set in a fictitious location. The model will accurately follow Great Western practice in all respects but because it is not a replica of a specific line it allows the modeller greater freedom of choice. Instead of having to restrict himself to the structures and scenic features of the specific station or line, he can select a station building, signal box, engine shed and other structures from various sites according to personal preference so long as they are appropriate to his layout. Modifications can also be made if desired to suit the situation on the model. In the same way, the scenic setting can be created as the modeller wishes provided the scenery is in keeping with the territory covered by the GWR. The resulting layout will have the style and character of a Great Western line and may well be more interesting and attractive than a model based more closely on a specific prototype line, as the features will have been selected for the best effect.

Another alternative is to choose an actual location where no line was built and to model the railway that might have been constructed there. This may be a completely imaginary railway company, as mentioned above in relation to freelance lines, but more often is based on one of the actual railway companies. The modeller might, for example, select a small town on the south coast not served by a railway and create his own Southern Railway branch line joining it

to a junction inland. His layout will feature a scenic setting based on the actual town and its surroundings and will follow Southern Railway practice but without the strict limitations of modelling a specific prototype line. Sometimes the modeller will base his layout on a line which was planned by one of the railway companies but which for one reason or another was never built. This approach combines the opportunity for interesting research with some freedom of design and planning in creating the line and also adds a degree of authenticity as a railway at this location was at least feasible enough to have been planned.

Some modellers like to create a detailed history for their railway and the district it serves, finding it an enjoyable and interesting sideline to the actual construction of the layout. That this is a useful as well as an entertaining exercise would seem to be borne out by the fact that some of the most believable layouts are ones for which this has been done. However, such a detailed scheme is not essential, although the enthusiast should have some idea in his mind of the background, real or imaginary, of the railway he is modelling if the result is to be convincing.

It is first necessary to decide where the railway is to be located. Though the British landscape does not show the extreme variations seen in some countries, for example the United States, there are definite differences between regions and correctly representing these characteristics is important in creating the right setting. These include not only the geological contours of the land but also the extent of woodland, the type of trees, the nature of the farming, the crops and livestock seen in the fields, the rivers, the local architecture and so on.

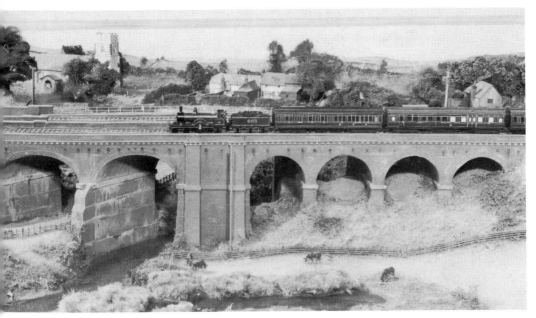

Superb modelling on the Model Railway Club's 2mm scale Chiltern Green layout has reproduced perfectly the characteristic undulation of the real countryside and the way the country buildings blend into the surrounding landscape (Len Weal).

We must also decide which railway company we are going to model. Which company built the line? Has it been taken over by another? Has it been nationalized? The railway companies, both before and after the grouping, had distinctive and recognizable features, many of which are still evident today, many years after nationalization, in the architectural style and the design of many other items. When correctly modelled, these will do a great deal to establish the right atmosphere for the scene.

We need also to decide what period in time we wish to represent on the layout. The design and liveries of the locomotives and rolling-stock, the styles of the costumes of the people and the types of road vehicles, together with many other small details, do much to set the date of a scene. Care must be taken to avoid anachronisms, particularly the introduction of anything that post-dates the period modelled.

We must also be clear in our minds why the railway is there and what its purpose is. Is it a branch line linking a small coastal town with the junction on the main line, with passenger and mixed freight services, boosted in the summer by holiday traffic? Was it built for a particular type of traffic such as coal, china clay, oil, livestock, etc? Is it a commuter line serving a large city?

Once we have a clear concept of why the railway exists and of its setting, we can start to plan a convincing model. For realism it is essential to consider the

This residential area on a large HO scale Fleischmann exhibition layout was created with kit-built houses, but the scene has been made more interesting by varying the ground level rather than modelling it completely flat.

scenery at the time that the track layout is planned. At this stage it is worth looking at the purpose of the scenic setting and how it can enhance the model railway.

The scenery on a layout provides an attractive setting for the trains and gives a realistic overall appearance. It can also make the layout appear larger and the length of run for the trains seem longer. By designing the scenery so that different areas of the layout are separated visually, these effects can be enhanced; it also gives more sense of purpose to operation, as the trains appear to be travelling from place to place through the model countryside rather than merely running round and round on a baseboard. The scenery, structures and

details also help to show the viewer what the geographical location of the railway is and give some idea of the period in which the model is supposed to be set. The scenery and structures also suggest the type of traffic which will be seen on the line, with the presence of a quarry, a mine or an oil depot, or of farms, a feed mill, a fertilizer plant and so on. The industries relate to the area modelled and enhance the impression of the geographical locale given by the scenery. Well-designed scenery will direct the eye of the viewer to areas of interest or activity, while concealing or disguising the compromises necessary because of limited space.

So we should not think of scenery merely as a fill-in to occupy the space on

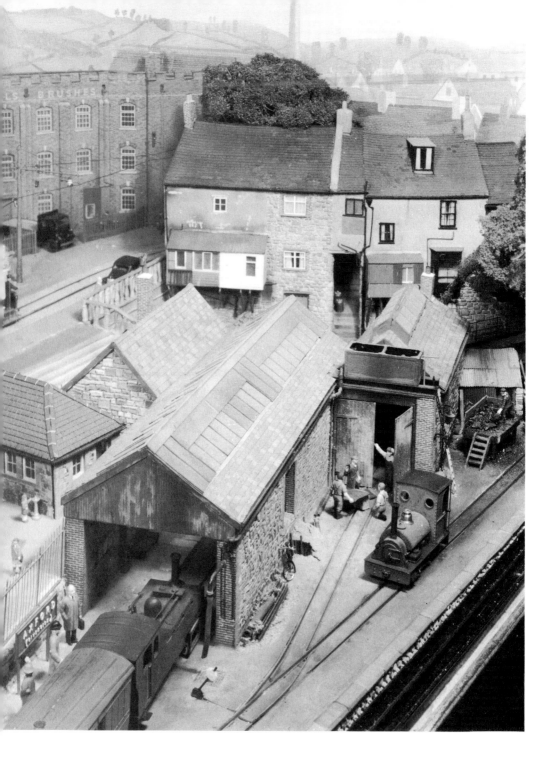

the baseboard not taken up by the railway. On the contrary, it should be regarded as a very positive way of enhancing the railway and helping to create a complete scene with the atmosphere of the real thing. To gain the maximum benefit possible, the scenery should be planned in conjuntion with the railway and not afterwards.

An important general principle in planning scenery is to get away from the flat toy-like effect which seems to be a hangover from the table-top model railway. There is a persisting tendency to work from the basis of a flat baseboard and for any differences in level to then be added on to this, with the result that these changes in height of the scenery are almost always upwards above the railway and there is still an overall impression of flatness. In fact, large flat areas are unusual in the British coun-

Left *Interesting structures and good grouping make this scene on Dave Rowe's 'Axford' layout realistic and natural in appearance. Note how the scenic background blends in with the models giving an impression of distance. The factory at the left rear is modelled in low relief. Note also the natural grouping of the railway workmen outside the door of the engine shed. The houses behind the station are based on prototypes in Lyme Regis and the factory is a model of one in Axminster* (Brian Monaghan).

Below *In Britain the ground is seldom completely flat even in towns and the buildings follow the contours as does this row of houses stepped up a slope. Note also the bracing supporting the partly collapsed wall.*

Mike Gill modelled these three houses in 4mm scale, and the sloping ground surface adds greatly to the interest and realism giving a very natural appearance. Note also the many small details including the window cleaner up a ladder and his motor-cycle and sidecar in the lane outside the house (Mike Gill).

tryside and much more often the landscape undulates, even in urban areas. For a realistic effect on a layout, the railway should be fairly level but the ground surface should rise above and fall below it.

The usual method of placing the track at the level of the top of the baseboard makes it difficult to extend the ground level below it. A better scheme is to have the lowest part of the landscape at baseboard level with the track supported above it at the appropriate height. Once you break away from the old flat scenic base scheme you will feel less constrained in your scenery modelling and this will result in a much more realistic terrain. It also means that cuttings, embank-

ments, bridges and tunnels can be realistically introduced on the layout. These are typical of prototype railways and are interesting in model form, but, because of the cost involved in construction, the real railways only built them when it was essential. Thus, for realism, when we include such features on a layout we must arrange our scenery so that they appear essential for our model rather than having been added just because they look interesting.

We may now consider how we can represent our chosen prototype realistically in model form. Most of us have only very restricted space which we can devote to the construction of a

An attractive scene on the Ilford & West Essex MRC 'Eastwell' 4mm scale EM gauge layout. The ground contours appear natural and make the bridge seem necessary (Len Weal).

model railway. Even if space is not a limiting factor, remember that it may still be wise to build a fairly small layout as the cost, work and time involved in the construction of a large model railway can be very considerable. Thus, though individual items, such as the locomotives and rolling-stock, structures, figures and details will be, of course, true-to-scale models, we must accept that we will not be able to reproduce the railway scene as a whole accurately to scale. Nor, indeed, would it be desirable to do so, as the result would probably not be very interesting.

Instead, we must create the illusion that the model is an accurate portrayal of reality while actually occupying a much reduced area. This requires an approach which is artistic and not mechanical and is accomplished by a combination of selection and compression. We must pick out those parts of the railway scene which we feel give it the individuality, character and atmosphere that we find interesting and attractive in the prototype. Features which are less interesting, are not very noticeable, are irrelevant or do not fit in with the impression we wish to give are omitted. With appropriate selectivity and with good modelling of the chosen elements, the scene will remain recognizable even though it may contain only a few key features.

We must also compress or foreshorten

the prototype to fit it into a feasible area, and this is made easier by the omissions we are making in condensing the scene. Bringing the essential parts closer together and more in relation to each other has the additional benefit of making the model more interesting to view. The form this compression takes will depend on the prototype, the space the modeller has at his disposal, and the effect he wishes to achieve. It will usually involve omitting some tracks or sidings and shortening other tracks, loops and platforms. It may include making a goods yard smaller, reducing the size of some structures and so on. The length of run must be drastically reduced, be it branch or main line, but this can be made less noticeable by using features such as bridges, tunnels, foreground trees and buildings to break up the onlooker's view of the line into several shorter segments rather than one longer continuous section. This form of optical illusion has the effect of making the line and the length of run for the trains appear longer, and it is also much more interesting for the viewer to see the train intermittently as it passes in and out of view.

The same principles of selection and compression are applied to the scenic setting for the railway. We cannot possibly duplicate the real landscape to scale in the space available so we must pick out the important parts of the scene that will make it recognizable for the area we are representing. Natural features such as mountains, lakes and rivers must all be made much smaller than scale, but if modelled well will appear realistic despite this.

In addition to selective compression, we should also plan how the features of the scenic setting can best be arranged to give a realistic and pleasing appearance. I would not perhaps go so far as to describe railway modelling as an art form, though I am sure a good case could be made to support that claim. However, there is increasing awareness among modellers that the principles of composition, form and balance as applied to art and photography also have some relevance in scenic modelling.

One of the ideas gaining favour is that the layout should be divided up into a number of separate but linked scenes, each of which acts as a centre of interest. Trees, buildings, hills and other features are arranged to separate these scenes visually so that the viewer is blocked from seeing them all at once, having thus to pause and study one scene fully before moving on to another. Breaking the layout up with 'view blockers' in this way makes it seem much larger and more interesting, and is a very effective technique for any layout, large or small.

Each scene should be interesting and well detailed to hold the viewer's attention. The areas between these centres of interest should be modelled to the same standard but will require less detail as they merely form link or transition areas which are not intended to attract attention away from the scenes.

We can further influence how the layout is viewed by restricting the gaze with blocks of various sorts; we can also direct the eye to parts of the layout we want to be noticed. Photographers often compose their pictures with lines leading in from the foreground to the subject; the eye of the viewer automatically follows these lines and is thus directed to the important part of the picture as the photographer intended. We can use a similar technique in scenic modelling. The track itself, a road, river,

Above *This beautifully modelled little scene on the Ilford & West Essex Model Railway Club 4mm scale EM gauge layout, 'Eastwell', is a good example of a small 'centre of interest' on a model railway. The viewer's eye will be held by such a scene studying all the details before moving on to look at other areas of the layout* (Len Weal).

Right *Attractive scenic work on the 4mm scale EM gauge 'Wigleton' layout built by Tony Hills. Here, the realistically modelled stream leads the eye to the horse and cart about to cross the bridge* (Len Weal).

In this scene on the H0 scale metre gauge Swiss prototype layout built by Mike and David Polglaze, the trees keep the viewer's gaze from straying away and the curved path leads the eye into the scene to where passengers are awaiting the arrival of a train.

fence, hedge or wall will all tend to lead the eye of the viewer into the scene from the foreground to reach the feature which you wish to emphasize. In the same way, such lines can be employed to link one centre of interest with another, leading the eye between them. The lines are especially pleasing if they are gently curved, breaking up the area in the scene and making it appear larger.

As in art and photography, our scenes should have balance and form. When developing a scene it is often helpful to try the structures in various positions before settling on the final arrangement. If the buildings have not yet been con-structed, use cardboard mock-ups; these need only be quite rough but will give you a good idea of the best placements. You may also find that the shapes of the proposed structures could be altered with advantage to the overall appearance and it is very helpful to know this before you have spent time on actual construc-tion. Some modellers like to make a mock-up of the scene or layout to a small scale to help them with planning and this can be very useful, particularly if the scene is to be a complex one. Again, following the example of art and photography, when placing a major structure within a scene position it a little to one side of the centre and balance it with a smaller building or other feature at the other side of the scene. This gives a better effect than if the larger building were placed dead centre. Just as the photographer often frames his subject with less important features around the edge of the picture, keeping the viewer's eye within the centre of the composition, so we can frame our scene with trees, buildings, hillsides or other features to prevent the eye from wandering too far. When adding detail to a scene, pause from time to time to study the effect and once the scene looks right don't be tempted to add more detail just for the sake of it; we want the scene to be well detailed as it will then look more realistic, but too much can become confusing and will spoil the overall appearance.

It is important to achieve a unified appearance, with the scenic setting blending harmoniously throughout and without any jarring features that look out of place. Consistency of standard is also important; individual models need only be of average standard but the quality throughout should be comparable. Models of a poorer finish will look out of place, while others with much more detail will make any nearby poorer models appear worse than they are; in either case the overall effect suffers.

Models in the foreground benefit from more detailing while those at the back of the layout can be simpler, but the impression to the viewer should be one of consistency.

We also need geographical similarity; scenes must blend naturally and realistically with one another without sudden changes which would be impossible in the real thing. If you want to model widely different scenic settings on the same layout, try to separate them completely visually by scenic dividers or blocks.

Colour and texture are also important in achieving a unified appearance throughout the layout. Using the earth colour employed for your scenery as the basis of weathering colours for track, structures and rolling-stock will give the impression that dust has blown on to everything and will help to tie the whole scene together in a natural and realistic way.

Take your time at the planning stage. It is the opportunity to try out many different arrangements and for these to inspire new ideas which you can develop at this time. It is much easier to make changes during the planning phase than once construction is under way, and your finished layout will be all the better if you have not rushed ahead too fast.

CHAPTER 5
Dioramas

The concept of modelling separate but linked scenes to act as centres of interest on a model railway layout, as outlined in the previous chapter, helps to display the areas in which you have put more work and effort into the modelling and detailing to the best possible advantage. The idea of diorama modelling, or what has been described as scenic module construction, fits well into this scheme. Military modellers, of course, very frequently present their models in the form

A view of a 4mm scale diorama scratch-built by Mike Gill. Careful choice of prototypes, excellent modelling with attention to detail, and good grouping have resulted in a natural and realistic scene. The structures show considerable variety but all blend harmoniously to create the desired overall effect (Mike Gill).

This attractive street scene was modelled in 4mm scale by Mike Gill. Construction as a diorama or module has allowed full detailing of the setting to be carried out, resulting in a very realistic appearance. Note the natural positioning of the figures (Mike Gill).

of dioramas of varying sizes, often with the individual scene having a theme or story to communicate to the viewer. The railway modeller can also benefit from this idea.

One way in which it can be applied is in the building up, section by section, of a complete layout. We do not need to have enough space for a layout to begin construction, but can instead build small parts, designed to link together to form a future layout, finishing each completely as we go. Later, when space is available, the separate sections can all be joined up. In this way a modeller can enjoy all aspects of construction work on the separate parts while also feeling that he is working productively all the time towards a complete layout.

The principle can also be applied very effectively to smaller units. When a structure, a factory building for example, is modelled, rather than placing it directly on to the layout it can be fitted

on to a small base which can then be scenically finished and detailed to create a small diorama. Because such a scene is relatively small and is easily accessible, you can make a really detailed and realistic setting in a comparatively short time. You can apply many small touches such as grass and weeds, scrap and rubbish, figures, fencing, barrels, crates, boxes and so on as appropriate. All parts of the model can be reached easily and you can work in comfort on your workbench or a table where the lighting will be good. The importance of this in achieving good results should not be underestimated; I find I work much more effectively at a table or workbench than when leaning uncomfortably over a layout trying to reach into a corner. Because a small diorama is so easy to handle you can also examine it from all angles easily and can ensure that it looks just right.

When the completed small scene is installed on the layout, it is easy to blend the surrounding scenery with the module. If you have several of these small scenes they can become centres of interest on the layout and the scenery between them can be modelled fairly easily and quickly as it will not need to be as detailed.

An advantage of this type of construction is that you do not need to have the layout ready to receive the modules before you build them. So long as you have some idea of what sort of structures or scenes you want, they can be built even before you start work on the layout, as the size of each module is only important insofar as it should be appropriate to the feature being modelled. Thus, a small structure may only require a diorama a few inches across whereas an industrial complex may need a much larger module. However, do try to avoid making them so large that you lose the advantages of easy handling and accessibility.

You do not need to build the whole layout as modules; they can make up only the centres of interest and can be linked by less detailed scenery constructed *in situ* on the layout. Remember that on

This engine repair and servicing area in 00 gauge has many small details making it interesting to view — note the numerous figures carrying out a variety of tasks. Mimmo Mattera built the scene as a diorama to be incorporated into a layout at a later date.

layouts built along a wall or walls it can be difficult to reach into the corners for scenery construction and detailing, so it is often much easier to make the scenery for each corner section as a separate unit on its own base, carrying out all the modelling on the workbench before fitting the scene into place. There is often sufficient space in these corners for fairly extensive scenic work and interesting features, and the full potential of these sites is much more likely to be realized if the modelling is done in separate units.

The modules can include track and, in fact, if there is any complex trackwork to be installed it can be more convenient to include it on modules like this rather than to attempt to fit it directly on to the layout, especially if access will be difficult. These units can then be linked by simple connecting tracks.

The beginner will find module building a very good way of starting. It provides experience and practice in all aspects of construction, scenery model-

Mike Gill built this interesting model of a builder's yard with its private siding as a diorama, making construction and detailing convenient and allowing the surroundings to be fully modelled. The scene is in 4mm scale (Mike Gill)

ling and painting, structure building, trackwork, detailing, weathering and so on. Any mistakes can be sorted out more easily on a small section on the workbench than on the layout itself. Building a small unit is quicker, easier and more likely to be successful, giving encouragement and confidence to the beginner and leading to the construction of further, more ambitious scenes. Before long he will be planning how they can be linked to form a layout!

The more experienced modeller will also find that modular construction has many advantages. The work can be carried out on the kitchen table if no space is available for a workshop or layout, so the enthusiast can enjoy some practical modelling in the construction of one or more units and later, if space does become available, part of the layout will already be built. In the meantime, he can take part in most aspects of layout construction, and the scenic modules once built can provide an excellent setting for the display of locomotives and rolling-stock.

Such dioramas are also very good for photography. They can be positioned and moved easily as required so that the best possible viewpoints and lighting can be achieved. It is easy to fit a background behind a diorama for photographic purposes; a sky backdrop can be mounted on a piece of hardboard or chipboard and this can then be supported temporarily in place. The modules also form an interesting setting for taking pictures of, for instance, locomotives, much better than merely placing them on a plain background. It is also easy to take the dioramas out of doors to take advantage of natural sunlight which often results in excellent pictures.

Their small size and ease of handling and carrying compared to even a small layout means that modules can be taken

This small coal mine is part of an 1830-era diorama built in HO scale by Malcolm Carlsson and has been photographed to good effect out of doors. The mine is based on the preserved late 18th-century mine at Coalbrookdale and is an interesting and attractive model with the atmosphere of the period. The locomotive is a Stephenson-type 2-2-2 tender locomotive from the North Cornwall Railway (Malcolm Carlsson).

to your local club or to exhibitions to show to other modellers or to be entered in competitions if you wish.

Another advantage is that if your layout is built up from a number of modules it is easier to make changes to your model. As your modelling standards improve, as they inevitably will with more practice and experience, you may find that your earlier modules are not up to the standards that you are now achieving, and it is fairly easy to cut round one or more and remove them. You can either upgrade such sections by adding extra details, or you can replace them altogether with new modules built to higher standards but occupying the same spaces. Alternatively, you may wish to change a scene completely, replacing a house with a factory, changing a coal yard into an oil depot, or whatever other alteration you would like to make.

If after a time you decide to scrap your present layout and build another, it is relatively easy and convenient to remove any modules intact for possible re-use. If necessary they can be modified, improved or updated quite conveniently before fitting them in place on the new layout.

Scenic modules also provide the opportunity for a little extra variety. You may already have a layout but become interested in or tempted by another scale, narrow instead of standard gauge, foreign rather than British, or a different period. By building one or more modules you can get the feel of the new scale or subject and can try it out without needing to neglect or scrap your present layout and without having to make too much commitment of time and money. Module construction is also an ideal way to experiment with different techniques or materials; if successful, they can be incorporated into your layout, but if not they can be scrapped without much inconvenience or expense.

For many reasons, then, the relatively new idea of building dioramas or scenic modules has much to recommend it to railway modellers. The accompanying photographs show several examples of small modules designed to be interesting in themselves but also planned so that they can later be incorporated into model railway layouts.

CHAPTER 6
Track

For realistic operation, our trains should run smoothly without faltering or derailing. In achieving this the importance of well-laid track giving smooth running and good electrical contact is self-evident, and accurate tracklaying should always be the aim of the railway modeller. However, in our efforts to achieve good operation we should not neglect the appearance of the track. When we come to consider the setting for our locomotives and rolling-stock, the track is one of the most important parts of the scene because it is so central to and noticeable on the layout. Wherever we look on a model railway some track will be in view, and wherever the locomotives and trains are they will have the track as their immediate setting. Structures and scenery are also often seen in close relation to the track, so whatever effort we put into making the track more realistic is likely to pay dividends in terms of overall realism.

I want to consider mainly 00 gauge track, though similar scenic treatment can of course also be applied to track in other scales. Unfortunately, for historical reasons, 4mm scale models are usually combined with 16.5mm (00) gauge track, an incorrect scale/gauge ratio. The standard prototype gauge of 4 ft $8\frac{1}{2}$ in should be modelled at 18.83mm at a scale of 4mm to 1 ft. Dissatisfaction with the incorrect scale/gauge ratio and the narrow gauge effect it produces has led some modellers to adopt the wider, more accurate EM gauge of 18.2mm, or the exactly correct P4/S4 gauge of 18.83mm. Now it must be acknowledged that these wider gauges do give a very realistic appearance as can be seen in some of the accompanying pictures. However, there is the difficulty that no ready-to-run motive power is available for either of these wider gauges, and although it is not too difficult to adapt ready-to-run 00 gauge models to EM or P4/S4, it does involve considerable extra work and expense.

Thus, for the majority of modellers 4mm scale on 16.5mm gauge is a standard that they must accept even though it is a compromise to strict accuracy, either because they do not want the complication of having to regauge purchased models or because they are too heavily committed already in terms of models and track to accept the work and expense involved in changing. Despite the incorrect scale/gauge ratio, there is much that can be done to give 00 gauge track a realistic appearance on the layout.

Many modellers will want to use the commercially available ready-made track for its convenience and good quality. Malcolm Carlsson, in an article in *Scale Model Trains,* made several in-

Right *Beautifully detailed scenic work on the Ilford & West Essex Model Railway Club's EM gauge 'Eastwell' layout. The track is very realistic and the lifted siding and point, the derelict lineside but with only the chimney left standing and the well-modelled weeds and ferns add greatly to the effect* (Len Weal).

Below *Realistically ballasted and weathered 00 gauge track on a Ratio display model. Note the lifted track in the left foreground and the pile of sleepers.*

teresting observations about ready-made 00 gauge track. The rail used in the track marketed by manufacturers such as Peco, Roco, Lima and Hornby is equivalent to code 100 flat bottom prototype rail which represents a heavier type of rail than that generally used in Britain. Because Peco track was designed for American HO scale use (3.5mm scale on 16.5mm gauge), the sleeper dimensions and spacing are not accurate for 4mm scale. The sleeper length of 29.5mm scales out to 7 ft 4½ in rather than 8 ft 6 in and the spacing should be 10mm not 7mm. He also points out that on many 00 gauge layouts the distance between track centres for parallel tracks is far too great. This is probably a result of the geometry of sectional track and ready-made points and of a concern to provide adequate clearances on curves. In fact, prototype track separation is a little over 11 ft centre to centre, and using 45mm in 4mm scale gives a much more realistic representation with a 'six-foot way' of 26mm, approximately 2mm overscale but with correct distances between the trains. He compares this with track centre to centre distances of 60mm often used, a six-foot way of 40mm.

Malcolm Carlsson has found that increasing the sleeper spacing to the correct 10mm by cutting the links between the sleepers and moving them to the new positions, discarding the surplus sleepers and laying the track to a correct track spacing produces a great improvement in appearance, as shown in the accompanying photographs. However, modifications of this type do involve a good deal of extra work and you may not wish to spend so much time and effort carrying them out. If you wish to use standard 00 gauge ready-made track without modification, do not be disheartened as there is

Peco track laid to 60mm centres giving a six-foot way of 40mm as quite commonly used on 00 gauge layouts. The heavy code 100 flat bottom rail is oversize though acceptable for modern British practice, but the sleepers are too short and too closely spaced for 4mm scale (Malcolm Carlsson).

still much that can be done in ballasting, colouring and weathering to give a realistic effect.

As bought, commercial track has sleepers that have an obvious plastic sheen and the rail is shiny, exaggerating its overscale heaviness. By the use of suitable colouring we can make the track appear much more realistic, and we can disguise some of the compromises we have already discussed. Track colouring varies with the age of the track, how much use it receives, the state of repair and the location. The rails and sleepers usually appear a dull brown colour, ex-

Standard code 100 flexible track modified by Malcolm Carlsson as described in the text to give correct sleeper spacing and laid at an accurate centre to centre measurement of 45mm. This produces a 26mm six–foot way, just 2mm over scale (due to the gauge error), but maintaining the correct separation between vehicles on adjacent tracks. The appearance is greatly improved. The track has also been ballasted, painted and weathered (Malcolm Carlsson).

cept for concrete sleepers which are grey and the tops of the rails which are shiny from use.

After pinning the track down it should be given an overall coat of dull matt brown. Humbrol Track Colour can be painted on, or alternatively a quick and easy method is to spray the track using the Precision Paints aerosol can of Track Colour (B112). Whether brushing or spraying, the paint should be kept off the contact rails in the points. The sleepers can then be drybrushed with slightly lighter shades of brown to give a weathered effect and to emphasise their wood grain appearance. Depending on the effect you want to achieve, the rails can be further coloured using a fine paint brush. For new rail, use a black/brown mixture to give a darker appearance, while for older rusty rails add rust colour to the black/brown mix, varying the proportions depending on how old and rusty you want the rails to look. The rust effect will be more noticeable on branch lines than on main line tracks, and most marked on sidings, particularly those seldom used. Once the painting is complete, remove any paint from the tops of the rails with a rail cleaner such as the Peco Track Rubber.

The next step is to ballast the track. The material employed is usually fine granite chippings or appropriately coloured cork granules. Whichever you choose be sure to use fine ballast. Often the particles in commercial products are considerably oversize and it is a good idea to use N scale ballast for 00 scale track.

I find the so called 'bonded ballast' technique devised in the United States to be the most satisfactory method for applying and fixing ballast. After the track has been laid, loose ballast is sprinkled along the track between and beside the rails. The ballast is then spread with a $\frac{1}{2}$ in wide brush, sweeping it away down to the level of the tops of the sleepers (take care to keep the ballast clear of all the moving parts of points). Spread it to achieve the appearance you want, making sure that there are no bare areas that need a little extra. Keep the ballast clear of the area where the wheels will run,

Two locomotives placed on the modified track show that there is still more than adequate clearance between them, provided sharp radius curves are not used. The Class '20' diesel on the left is the Lima version, depicted here during upgrading to a super detailed model (Malcolm Carlsson).

especially between the rails and check rails. Once it all looks right, the ballast is sprayed with water containing a few drops of a detergent, such as washing-up liquid; this is easily done with a water sprayer of the type intended for watering houseplants and available at garden centres and many other shops. Set the sprayer to give a fine mist of water and spray from far enough away to ensure that the ballast will not be blown out of position. Spray the track 2 or 3 ft at a time and make sure that the ballast is thoroughly soaked and that you have not wet only the top surface. Then apply drops of a solution of 1 part acrylic matte medium (available from art shops) to 3

parts water; alternatively, use diluted white glue in the same way. The drops can be applied using an eye-dropper, but a rather quicker and easier method is to use a soft plastic bottle as it will hold more. The drops spread easily through the ballast due to the previous damping with the detergent solution.

When the process is completed, leave it to dry overnight and then gently brush off any loose ballast. If there are any areas which need touching up with a little extra ballast, add it now and repeat the spraying and application of the adhesive. Carefully remove any ballast or adhesive which has stuck to the running surfaces of the rails. As mentioned above, diluted white glue can be employed as an alternative to the acrylic matte medium; however, the glue dries hard whereas the matte medium remains more flexible and resilient, giving a useful cushioning effect.

The completed track will benefit from some weathering to make it appear more natural and realistic, and this is where observation of the prototype becomes especially important. Colour photographs of track are particularly useful as a guide to getting the right effect. If the ballast on your completed track appears too bright, apply a thin wash of earth colour to give a dusty appearance and

realistically tone down the original colour. Often there are black stains from oil and grease dripping on to the ballast, typically along the centre of the track; this is even more marked over and around the track at diesel maintenance areas. Oil and grease also spread on to the track around points, and thinned black paint brushed on to the ballast and sleepers can be used to represent them; alternatively you can gently brush on a little black powdered pastel chalk to give the same effect. You will also find that some rust spreads onto the track from the rails, mainly on the outer side, and this is well represented by thin-

This old coach beside the tracks was built from a Ratio kit and has been very realistically weathered. Note the broken windows, other windows boarded up and the 'keep out' notice crudely painted on the side.

This trackside shed was built from a Ratio 4mm scale kit by Derek Purkis. Note the realistic weathering with rain-streaked dirt on the roof.

ned rust coloured paint or by appropriately coloured powdered pastel chalk.

Spillage or dust blowing from loads carried by freight trains can also colour the track, black from coal dust, red from iron ore, white from limestone or cement, and so on, and these can all be simulated with paint or powder colour. If your railway operates steam locomotives, there will be a coal spilled around the coaling stage. Finally, puddles of water or damp areas alongside the track where the engines take on water can be represented by painting on a little clear gloss varnish.

Many sidings have grass and weeds growing on them, particularly if they are seldom used. This can be represented in model form with coarse turf texture material, string fibres or brush hairs coloured with a dull yellow-green paint. Where these are applied between the rails, keep them short so that they do not interfere with the trains passing over the tracks. On sidings, especially little-used factory tracks, you will often see all sorts of scrap and rubbish lying around and this can be realistically modelled. Scrap wood, old boxes and crates, rusty scrap iron and corrugated iron sheet, broken glass (which can be modelled with thin clear plastic), paper and so on. Glue down the various items, making sure that none of them will foul the trains using the tracks.

There are also many lineside details which can be added to make the track appear more interesting and realistic. Some are available commercially as detail items, while others can be scratch-built quite easily. They include dummy point levers, point rodding, electric point motors and ATC (Automatic Train Control) ramps. Boxes for relays and other electrical equipment are often seen at the trackside, as are ballast bins, small huts, pieces of rail and other track parts, and numerous signs and notices of various types.

This scene on a Ratio exhibition module combines realistic track with a variety of typical lineside details, signal, ground signal, loading gauge, fencing and an old coach used as a trackside store, all creating a very effective result.

CHAPTER 7
Detailing diesels
by Chris Ellis

The days are long gone when most railway modellers thought only in terms of steam locomotive models and regarded diesel models as modern interlopers not worthy of attention. In fact, diesel traction now has a respectable history of its own going back over fifty years in the United States and in mainland Europe, though in Great Britain most of the development has been in the last thirty years or so. Nonetheless, there were diesel shunters and railcars in Britain even in the 1930s, so the vintage period modeller could quite justifiably include suitable diesel traction on a pre-1948 layout.

The diesel locomotive has now come of age, and a whole generation of young modellers has grown up in the diesel age without having experienced steam traction except on preserved lines. In addition, many older modellers who once thought only in steam terms have since found a fascination for diesels and have switched their interest, and there is a popular following for the steam-diesel transition period of about 1959-1965 where the modeller can have the best of both worlds at a time which is also now far enough off to have a distinct period flavour quite unlike today's railway scene.

If you are new to the idea of diesel modelling, you might note the gleaming models by Hornby, Lima and others in the window of your local hobbyshop and think that they look pretty good as they come. This is true, they do. Most models represent a good likeness to the prototype and are good value for money. But the seeker after something even better can have a fine time working over almost any model and refining it, sometimes even converting it, to arrive at a model with much more individuality than it had when it left the manufacturer's production line. If you take almost any diesel locomotive model straight from the box, place it on a length of track and compare it with a photograph of the full-size locomotive, you will see what I mean. Study the model from eye level or from the same angle as the prototype photograph. Scan it slowly from end to end and you are bound to spot at the very least some detail omissions or discrepancies on the model.

Look at the cab windows. Are they deeply recessed? Are the screen wipers depicted? Look at the buffer beams. Are the buffers too small? Are the brake pipes

A recent model, the Lima Class '37', needs little extra work in its BR blue form. This one has a new nameplate, a driver in each cab, big coupler replaced with the small Airfix type, added brake/heat pipes on the coupler sides (so that they swing with it), and light weathering. Note the dry-brushed detail on the bogie sides and exhaust staining on the roof (Chris Ellis).

Class '73' for British Rail, an Atlas 'RS-3' or Athearn 'GP3B' for the United States, or almost any Roco model of your choice for Continental Europe. With any of these you are getting quality and good performance, and any extra work you do on the model will be well rewarded. If you don't already have any books on diesels, familiarize yourself with them by borrowing some from the public library. Similarly, acquire any magazines you can find with relevant features; there are several dealing with prototype railways which will yield many pictures and useful background details. Start a cuttings file if you can, or best of all read the model railway magazines where frequent 'how to do it' articles on detailing specific diesel locomotive models are published. *Scale Model Trains,* for example, has a diesel detailing project in almost every issue. Immersing yourself in the subject is important as you will then acquire a good idea of what to look for in the way of class variations and

detail fittings. Note that modern models, such as the Lima Class '37', may actually need 'back dating' in detail terms if you wish to accurately depict the 1960s prototype appearance, as today's models represent the 1980s fittings.

The related 'golden rule' to all this research is to work always with at least one picture, preferably more, of the actual individual locomotive you want to model, since subtle detail variations can occur from locomotive to locomotive throughout a class. You may, for example, wish to detail a Class '47' model; if you choose a number at random to apply to the model, you could be in trouble from the point of view of strict accuracy. The number you have chosen may belong to a locomotive with a different colour scheme, or with different front end fittings. The number may even be one missing from the series, that is a locomotive that does not actually exist. So don't ever be tempted to guess if you want to achieve the best possible results.

Typical detailing on the older Hornby Class '37' is let down by inaccurate bogies. Here the bogie detail has been corrected with foot steps in the right position, brake cylinders and wiring (from fine fuse wire) added, and the belly tanks have been extended to scale length and detailed with filler caps etc. The wheels have been blackened and completely new decals have been applied to change its identity (Chris Ellis).

Tools and materials

The good news here is that for diesel detailing you need only the simplest of tools. A small craft knife or scalpel, flat and round files of the 'needle' type, an emery-board, 'wet and dry' paper, a razor saw, a small screwdriver, a pin-vice and some small drill bits will suffice. A Minidrill instead of the pin-vice would be an added luxury if you have one.

The materials required are also easy to come by. Plastic card sheet in 10, 20, 30, 40, and 60 thou thickness is always useful. In addition, we will need paper or card punchings or an office punch to make them with, plastic filler or Milliput, ordinary card and paper and handrail wire. A very useful item is the No 56 size office staple and the smaller size Bambi staple, plus pliers to cut and bend them. The staples are available cheaply from any stationer and a packet provides vir-

tually a lifetime's supply. Being of flat section, these staples are ideal for modern diesel handrails, and can also be cut and bent to make screen wipers, radio aerials, lamp irons, stirrup-type steps and other fittings. You won't want to be without them once you have seen how handy they are.

Lastly there should be a 'spares box' in your inventory somewhere. Save all sorts of bits and pieces and useful shapes as they may all come in handy eventually. Any parts removed from one model should be saved for possible future use on others, and even 'junk' items can be useful. Small headlights saved from plastic car kits, for example, are ideal for diesel headlights if of a suitable size. Similarly, I have used seats left over from truck kits as cab seats in diesel locomotives.

You will need figures too; although seated figures of drivers are available,

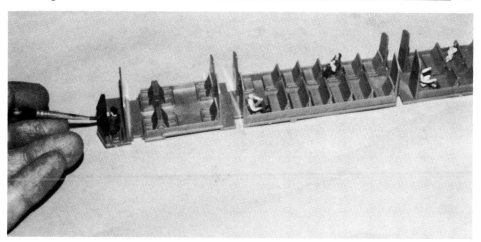

Painting a DMU interior and adding passengers and a driver (Chris Ellis).

you can often adapt and repaint suitable seated passenger figures as an alternative. For diesel railcar or multiple unit sets, you will need to add seated passengers inside; it is remarkable just how much better a DMU looks if miniature passengers can be seen riding inside, and a driver visible in the cab of

This close-up view of a Hornby DMU shows added passengers (note newspaper glued to hands), painted seats and 'no smoking' signs from SMS decal sheets. The wheels have been replaced with Ultrascale fine scale wheels and the underframe has been weathered (Chris Ellis).

This front view of the Hornby DMU shows added driver, dead irons, lamp irons, cab steps and heat and brake pipes (from bell wire), together with a scale coupling. The model is seen before painting so that the additions can be seen (Chris Ellis).

any diesel unit really brings it to life. In British and Continental diesels, I place a driver in each cab of a double-ended locomotive, and the figure in the trailing cab then depicts the guard. It is worth pointing out at this stage that Roco produce a set of 'head and shoulders only' drivers which are useful for those models where the cab is occupied by the motor bogie so that full cab detail cannot be fitted. In these models, the 'head and shoulders' figure can be cemented in at window level to show the presence of a driver even though there is not room for all of him.

Detailing kits

In the last few years, many kits have been issued for detailing and converting ready-to-run diesel locomotive models, and Shawplan, Crownline, Westward, and Cambrian are among the names to look for. They also produce all the detail parts separately, such as screen wipers and horns, and for American models Details West/Detail Associates offer a comprehensive range of detail parts. The detailing kits come with a mix of cast metal and brass etched parts and there is almost always a good instruction sheet. Sometimes, however, this does not give all the information you need, so resort to your own references as well.

These detailing kits certainly make conversion and detailing easy because they save you a lot of time and trouble by providing all the required components in a single package. Some of the more elaborate kits are quite expensive, however, sometimes costing nearly as much as the basic model they are designed to complement, so whether or not you employ the kits or do all your detailing using scrap items is a matter for you to decide for yourself, perhaps influenced by your modelling budget. There are

Above *An old mill modelled in 4mm scale by Mike Gill. Note how the building has been set into the ground surface and has been realistically weathered to give the appearance of a structure which has been standing for many years* (Peco).

Below *The 'Railway Hotel', a typical country pub skilfully modelled in 4mm scale by Mike Gill. The many details including figures, flowers, tables with glasses and the garden fork outside the conservatory add greatly to the scene* (Peco).

Left and below left *Two attractive scenes on a 4mm scale exhibition module featuring Ratio plastic kit models. Excellent modelling and attention to both the overall effect and the small details has created a very realistic impression of a Great Western branch line.*

Above right and right *Two prototype tank wagons showing typical weathering patterns. The Esso tanker is generally grimy — note how the rain has streaked the dirt in a downward direction on the tank. The markings have been wiped clean to keep them visible and legible while those on the chassis appear to have been repainted for the same reason. Note the grass growing on the track in the foreground. The ICI tank wagon shows white chemical spillage down the body and on the chassis, easily represented on a model with matt white paint.*

Above *Dioramas are ideal for photographic purposes and are particularly convenient for trying out special effects. A small diorama with an 009 locomotive and its train of wagons crossing a girder bridge was positioned in front of a back-projected 35mm colour transparency taken on holiday to produce this dramatic silhouette.*

Below *Even a very simple base together with a backscene can provide an effective setting for photographing model locomotives and rolling stock. This Midland Railway 2-4-0 in 4mm scale, built from a Ratio kit, was posed in front of a Faller scenic background. The low viewpoint adds to the realism.*

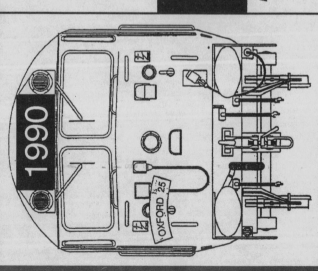

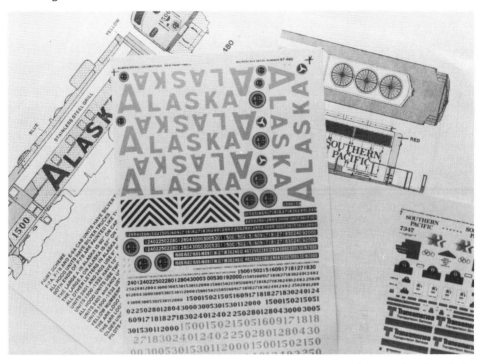

Above *Typical of decal sheets available for diesels is Micro-scale's sheet for the Alaska Railroad and a smaller N scale sheet for Southern Pacific finish* (Chris Ellis).

Below *The inexpensive Bachmann H0 scale 'GP40' correctly detailed and repainted to depict an actual Cotton Belt locomotive of around 1979. The decals are from Microscale sheets* (Chris Ellis).

A Graham Farish N gauge Class '47' with weathering, footsteps added on the buffer beams and the wheels blackened. Minor improvements like this are possible even with N gauge models (Chris Ellis).

stippling with an almost dry paintbrush, is a great way to bring up surface detail on dark painted chassis and underframes. Using a chisel brush only very lightly loaded, you can add streaks by rainstrips etc to depict rain runs. Similarly, some light streaky weathering on bogie sides and the belly tanks will indicate a lot of running.

If in doubt, however, it is better to leave the model 'ex-works' and pretend it is freshly outshopped rather than do a clumsy job of weathering. If you are un-

sure, use the new acrylic water-soluble paints now available; their advantage is that if you do not like the results of your handiwork you can quickly wash off the paint and start again. The pictures in this section show some typical detailing and converting projects and demonstrate the work that goes into a typical model. Don't hesitate — if you have not yet tried diesel detailing, do have a go. It's much more fun than 'straight from the box' modelling.

CHAPTER 8
Weathering

Of the many developments and innovations that have taken place in railway modelling, one of the most significant in terms of realism has been the concept of weathering. At one time all model locomotives were finished as though they had just emerged from the paint shop and care was taken to match the colours as exactly as possible to the actual paint colours used on the real engines. However, perceptive modellers who looked at the real locomotives in action as part of the whole railway scene realized that models operating on a model railway layout and finished in this way did not accurately portray the real thing.

One of the reasons is that real locomotives soon show the effects of the weather, with dirt and dust being blown on to them and then being streaked by rain, with touches of rust appearing and so on. Painting locomotives to represent these effects was found to add considerably to their realism, and the term 'weathering' came into use to describe this technique. However, there is a good deal more than merely the effects of the weather involved in the concept of modifying the colour and finish of locomotives to give a more realistic representation of how they actually look

in service. The principles also apply to rolling-stock, structures and even scenery, and have found wide application in other branches of modelling, particularly military modelling.

There are several reasons why painting a model in exact prototype colours is not realistic. One is the different light intensity under which the prototype and the model are viewed. The real thing is seen outdoors illuminated by sunlight or diffuse daylight which is many times brighter than the lighting on even the best lit of indoor layouts (and many layouts are, in fact, rather poorly lit). To see form and shape properly, we must be able to see shade and shadows and the details within them. The bright light outdoors creates this effect even with a black-painted locomotive, but if we paint a model black and place it on a layout with much weaker indoor illumination it will appear with an unrelieved black colour all over and we will lose much or all of the form and details within the shadows. To overcome this, black locomotives should always be painted a dark grey rather than black. If 10-20% white is added to the black paint, a suitable model locomotive black colour will be produced. In fact, all model colours will benefit from some lightening with white or grey to allow for this difference in illumination intensity.

Outdoors there is also atmospheric dilution of colours due to haze and fine dust particles in the air, causing a dulling, muting and greying of the colours of distant objects; the greater the distance, the more intense the effect. The distances at which we view models on a layout correspond to seeing the prototype at a moderate distance and we thus need to represent this atmospheric effect on the colours to give the correct overall appearance on the layout. Another factor to be taken into consideration is that even if the prototype has a gloss finish, because of the distances at which it is normally viewed compared to those at which we view the scaled-down model, the gloss finish will not be evident, so models should normally be painted in matt colours.

These principles apply to any model, even one which is to represent a newly-painted prototype locomotive or item of rolling-stock just beginning service. The comments above about adding white or grey to the basic paint colour apply when you are painting any locomotive or rolling-stock model, whether it is scratch-built, kit-built or a ready-to-run example which you are repainting. For ready-to-run models with a satisfactory finish which you do not intend to re-paint, this toning down and lightening of the basic colours can be carried out as part of the general weathering process.

We now come to weathering in the sense of representing the effects of climate and conditions on equipment and structures. We need to simulate fading and bleaching of paintwork, rusting of metal parts, deposits of grime,

dust, mud and oil to a greater or lesser degree depending on the state of the prototype. Various methods and materials have been successfully employed and you can choose whichever you prefer, use whatever combination you like, or develop your own individual technique. One essential for success is, as always, careful observation of the prototype.

One effective method of weathering is the use of paints. These can be the usual modelling paints such as Humbrol or Floquil; the latter firm produces a special range of colours designed for weathering purposes including Dust, Grime, Mud and Rust. A very convenient alternative is acrylic paint, available as tubes of artists' colours at art supply shops. These have the advantage of being water soluble and are easy to use. Black, white and brown are the essential basic colours but it can also be useful to have light brown, grey and yellow in your selection. Various painting techniques can be employed, separately or in combination to give an effective weathered finish.

Thin washes of paint can be used to give an overall dusty and dirty appearance. These can be the commercially prepared weathering colours such as Floquil Dust or Grime, or can be made up from black, brown, grey or other colours to suit your requirements. The paint should be applied so that the brush strokes are vertically downwards in the direction that rain water would run and cause streaking of the dust, grime and dirt already present. The paint will collect in crevices and corners and on ledges and other protrusions, just as dirt and dust would accumulate on the prototype. If there is rather too much paint you can wipe some of it off with a paper tissue while it is still wet; this gives an effective grimy and streaked ap-

Typical weathering on a prototype wagon. Note the peeling paint, the repainted identification panels and the relatively light colour of the chassis.

pearance with more paint left in the corners. You may need to apply the paint unthinned in some areas, as for example the underframes, bogies, axle-boxes and wheels on prototype stock which are often surprisingly light in colour whereas on ready-to-run models they are frequently black. An overall coat of a light dusty brown will be a good basis for these areas on a model, followed by a thin wash of black to emphasize the details and a final touch of a little highlighting of projecting details using the dry-brushing technique.

Patches of rust may also be represented with unthinned paint. Rust varies considerably in colour, so look at

the real thing and try to introduce these variations in tone on your models. The rust colours provided in the paint ranges are often rather too bright and will benefit from toning down with a little black. The insides of wagons will collect a good deal of dirt but the colour will also be influenced by the loads carried, whether coal, iron ore, china clay, stone or whatever. An overall wash of an appropriate colour can be applied to the interior together with additional unthinned paint to give more colour on the floor and in the corners.

The dry-brushing technique is also very effective in weathering. Using a slightly lighter shade than the basic weathering coat, the brush is dipped into

This scratchbuilt mineral plant on Peter Gentle's 3mm scale 'Mullion' layout is closely modelled on a real structure in Cornwall. The carefully simulated dusty and weathered appearance enhances the realism of this interesting model.

tually enhance the details on the surface of the model by making them more visible. Also be subtle in the colours and blend them together in a natural way. It is always better to do too little rather than to overdo the weathering; part of the art is knowing when to stop!

CHAPTER 9
Structures

The structures on a model railway layout are very important as they add interest and realism and also help to provide visible evidence of the purpose of the railway and the reason it was built. In addition to the purely railway-related buildings, such as stations, goods sheds, engine sheds and signal cabins, there are houses, cottages, shops, farms and many other types of commercial and industrial structures which can be modelled. Model buildings not only make a layout more interesting to view but also contribute to the overall effect by reinforcing the impression of geographical location in the choice of prototypes appropriate to the area being portrayed. The construction materials represented and the architectural styles of the houses and other buildings, the types of industry, whether the buildings are well maintained or neglected, even derelict — all these factors influence atmosphere and realism. Model structures are always noticed by viewers and form centres of interest within a scene.

The buildings on your layout can therefore be very important. Also structure modelling can be a very enjoyable part of the hobby and it is one in which the beginner may find an excellent in-troduction to constructional work. Because the resulting models do not have to 'operate', accuracy in modelling can be less critical than it is in the construction of locomotives and rolling-stock, whether from kits or from scratch, and the beginner is more likely to end up with a satisfactory model. This is not to say that every effort should not be made to achieve the best possible results; the more realistic the structures, the better the overall appearance of the layout, and standards will quickly improve with practice.

I do not want to consider the actual construction techniques of structure modelling here, whether from card, plastic or other kits, or from scratch. This has been dealt with in some detail in PSL's *Model Railway Guide 3 — Structure Modelling.* Instead I want to look at various ways in which we can gain the maximum benefit in terms of overall realism from our structure models.

The choice of the structures for a layout is very important. They must be selected not only for their individual appeal but for how well they will contribute to the overall effect. To create a realistic appearance it is essential that our buildings are not just an unrelated collection of models but blend naturally together to form a harmonious whole. This requires careful planning and you must also be prepared to leave out any structure, however attractive, if it does not fit into this overall scheme.

As discussed in Chapter 4, your layout, even if not modelled on a specific prototype line, will probably be based on a more or less specific geographical location, and the buildings chosen should be appropriate in architectural style and building materials for that area. This is where research into the area you are

Dave and Shirley Rowe's latest modelling project is this fine diorama 'Exebridge Quay'. Note the beautifully modelled structures, the many small details, the low-relief building at the rear and the realistic scenic backdrop (Dave Rowe).

The Ratio 4mm scale water tower kit assembles into a very nicely detailed model and its realism has been enhanced in this scene by careful weathering and by bedding it down into the ground surface so that it blends in perfectly with its surroundings.

planning to model, whether in the form of personal visits or the study of books and magazines, will be helpful in finding suitable prototypes. Because most layouts are fairly limited in size and therefore only provide space for relatively few structures, we should be quite selective and choose buildings which are attractive and interesting; they should also preferably be fairly small structures. Because there is such a wide variety of prototype structures, we can, by appropriate selection, give the layout great individuality by the choice of model buildings.

While there are a number of structure kits available, the choice is limited and because many of the models are designed for general situations on any layout they tend not to be ideal for a specific site. One also loses the opportunity to make the layout different and interesting by virtue of its unique buildings. It is generally best therefore to scratch-build structures for a layout, or at least to modify considerably any kits employed.

One of the key factors in achieving a good overall appearance is consistency in the modelling and presentation throughout the layout. The different structures should be built from the same materials (for example card with brick-paper, or embossed plastic sheet, or individually laid bricks from computer punchings, etc) and to the same standard. Even if the models are not particularly well detailed they will look much better with this even standard throughout than if some are poorly constructed and others are super-detailed.

Structures near the front of the layout can have extra detailing while those at the rear can be more simple, but the overall effect should still be one of consistency. The degree of texture of the surfaces, and the extent of detailing on the buildings should also be similar throughout. If you do use kit models, they should be finished by painting, weathering and detailing, so that card, plastic or other kit models and scratch-built structures all appear to be the same in construction. Small details, such as the chimney pots, guttering and down-pipes in the Scalelink range, can do a great deal to enhance the appearance of structure models.

The way the buildings are arranged on the layout is very important in creating a realistic and visually attractive grouping. This is easier to achieve if you plan all the structures for your layout at an early stage rather than adding them bit by bit. A useful method is to make rough mock-up models of the structures you plan to include in the scene from scrap card. These dummies can be tried in various positions and groupings until you find the one you like best. Creating some variation in ground level throughout the scene with different buildings at varying heights will often make for a much more interesting and realistic appearance than if everything is dead flat. With the rough mock-up models you may find that alterations to some of the structures would give a better overall effect; it is obviously an advantage to find this out before you have built the actual models.

For realism it is essential that model structures are properly bedded into the ground with no unsightly crack or gap visible between the base of the building and the ground surface. One method is to build the model with the walls exten-ding perhaps half an inch below ground level and then fit it into a rectangular (or other appropriately shaped) hole cut out of the ground; any gap is thus much less visible, being vertically placed instead of horizontally, and it is easily concealed with a little filler or texture material. Another approach is to build each structure, or group of structures, on a separate base, as discussed for dioramas (Chapter 5). The building is fixed down firmly to this base and any cracks between the two are filled in with plaster or filler, then painted and finished with a little texture material to competely cover the join. The base is then built into the layout. This method has the advantage that the surrounding area can be fully scenically detailed on the workbench before having to fit it into the layout. Structures are greatly enhanced by the addition of many small details, perhaps together with human or animal figures, and considerable attention should be paid to the setting in gaining maximum realism.

These general remarks so far apply to all types of structures, but I would now like to briefly consider the modelling of industrial buildings. Such structures have the advantage of not only providing scenic interest but also of giving the opportunity for increasing the operating scope of the line. These industries need sidings to serve them, with a resulting increase in shunting activity, and they will generate extra goods traffic over the whole railway. They may also enable us to run unusual or special items of rolling-stock associated with particular industries. Another advantage for the railway modeller is that older industrial areas are often crowded and cramped, with buildings close together and with sharp curves in the tracks serving their factories and warehouses. In modelling such an area, the limited space we have available and the sharp curves we must therefore use will appear more realistic than if we were representing a rural line.

Even if your layout is a model of a country branch line, one or two small industries such as a factory, a warehouse, a dairy or an oil depot can usually be accommodated realistically. Alternatively, a very interesting shunting layout based entirely on one industry, on a variety of different industries or on a dock area can be built to provide considerable operating scope in a small area. Such a layout can also keep the modeller enjoyably occupied for a long time finding suitable prototype structures and modelling and detailing them, as a considerable number of buildings can be included.

Despite all these advantages, industrial buildings are often rather neglected by

A very effective industrial scene on the Ilford & West Essex MRC EM gauge layout. The scrap metal has been most realistically modelled and the narrow gauge track complete with small crane adds interest to the model.

This realistically modelled small boatbuilder's yard is an interesting and attractive small industrial structure on the Ipsley Circle's 4mm scale 'Coombe Mellin' layout. Note the boat under construction inside the shed.

railway modellers, either being ignored altogether or being represented only by rather stereotyped and not very realistic models. This may be because they do not have details of suitable prototypes or because they feel that industrial structures are too large to model satisfactorily on a small layout. In fact, if you look around there are many small prototype industrial buildings packed with interesting details which are ideal for modelling purposes. Even structures which are rather too large can often be selectively compressed to fit on to a layout without dwarfing the surrounding features. The secret is to choose the important characteristic features of the industry which distinguish it from others. If we take a gasworks as an example, we must include a gasholder, but only one rather than two or more as in the prototype, and we need only model some of the other buildings making up the whole complex. The result is a recognizable and apparently realistic gasworks but in a very much smaller space than would be required for an accurately scaled model. In addition to leaving out some of the less important or duplicated features, the structures can also be compressed in size to some extent without spoiling the effect. One method is to model the buildings to a slightly smaller scale, say H0 instead of 00, particularly if they are to be at the back of the layout. A reduction in size can also be achieved without loss of the general effect and appearance by leaving out one or more storeys of tall buildings, reducing the length by omitting some of the windows or bays, making windows smaller (but not doors or doorways) and so on. Another useful technique is to model some or all of the structures in low relief.

As always, for realistic results you are

Above *This colliery which is one of the exhibits at the Beamish Museum is small enough to be modelled realistically on even a small layout and would be an interesting and authentic feature.*

Below *Part of a Cornish tin mine modelled in 4mm scale by Steve Dewhirst. This authentic model was built from scratch and forms the central feature of an 009 layout. Like the coal mine, this is one of many industries which can be realistically included on model railway layouts.*

A derelict cottage realistically modelled by Mike Gill in 4mm scale. Note the plaster breaking away from the brick, the collapsed roof to the extension and the broken window (Mike Gill).

represented quite simply. For a wooden surface, apply a coat of pale grey, allow to dry thoroughly and then dab on patches of rubber cement or Maskol. After this has dried, paint on the required colour for the structure and again allow it to dry. The rubber cement or Maskol can now be peeled off and you will be left with peeled paint with realistic frayed edges and the bare weathered wood showing through. For metal areas, the first coat should either represent undercoat or rust; the peeled areas are treated as for the wood surface, but the result will be areas of undercoat or patches of rust exposed.

CHAPTER 10
Scenic backgrounds

In adding realism to a model railway, the *overall* effect is very important. We are building a scenic setting which we hope will give the impression of the real landscape. However, most of us have strictly limited space in which to create this illusion and much of the effect of our scenic work will be lost if, when the eye of the viewer travels to the back of the modelled landscape, it abruptly encounters real wallpaper, curtains and furniture behind the layout! We need some means of extending the apparent depth of our scene into the distance as far as the eye can see, and the answer is to provide a scenic background. Even a very simple backscene will give a remarkable improvement in the appearance and realism of a layout.

There are several benefits from adding a scenic background, and the time, work and expense involved will be more than repaid by these advantages. Merely blocking out the distracting features behind the layout such as patterned

This American commercially-produced backscene gives the impression of great distance on the N scale 'Dabble Creek & Greenfield Railroad' layout built by Bill Fellows.

Above *Pennington station on Colin Woolridge's 2mm scale narrow gauge layout. The locomotive is based on two Marklin Z gauge chassis regauged from 6.5mm to 5mm to represent a 2'6" gauge prototype and the wagons are also modified Marklin models. The scenic background has been realistically blended with the modelled scenery and makes the layout appear much larger than it actually is.*

Below *Rugged mountainous scenery provided by an MZZ scenic background gives the finishing touch to this Swiss village modelled in H0 scale. This range of backscenes is produced in Switzerland and is available in Britain from Swiss Trains of Aberdeen (Swiss Trains).*

wallpaper, windows, doors, furniture and curtains will help to keep the viewer's attention focused on the model. This is even more noticeable in photographs where such items intruding into view can make the pictures very confusing; here even a plain white background is a significant improvement. A well-designed scenic background can not only complete the scene, it is also very useful for concealing a fiddle yard or other hidden tracks or sidings, giving a complete scenic break between the visible and concealed tracks in a minimum of depth.

Backscenes are generally employed at the rear of a layout but can also be employed along one, two or even three sides of a rectangular layout, and as layout dividers to separate a rectangular layout into two halves. This is especially suitable if hills or mountains can be situated in the central part of the layout, but can also work well with other terrain, or even an urban setting. Such a central divider can be a double-sided backscene providing a background for each side of the layout, a very good scheme as it makes the 'round and round' nature of the usual oval or figure of eight track plan much less obvious as well as adding to the realism both scenically and operationally by creating the impression of two separate areas between which the trains run. The central divider may occupy only the centre of the oval or can be extended further to divide the layout into two completely separate sides, a useful arrangement for a layout operated by two enthusiasts together.

I have seen this idea taken even further on a Z scale layout, the 'Western Pacific' built by Bruce Goehmann and described in a series of articles in the American magazine *Model Railroader* in 1986. This layout is completely divided scenically into four parts, each of which features quite different scenery — a river canyon, Californian hill country, Nevada desert, and a city scene. The model is very effective and has given the builder the opportunity to model scenes he finds particularly attractive and interesting, but which are located far apart in reality, on the same layout without compromising its realism. Finally, on an exhibition layout a scenic background can be fitted to conceal a central operating well.

There are two important considerations in installing a scenic background; firstly the backscene itself and secondly the blending of the two-dimensional background with the modelled scenery of the foreground.

Most modellers use commercially-produced backscenes for their model railways and we will look at these in detail a little later on. One criticism of these products is that the same scenes appear on many other layouts and some modellers prefer to create their own individual scenic backgrounds, designed for and unique to their own layouts.

One method of creating a backscene is to use selected colour pictures. At one time, travel and other posters were popular as backgrounds for model railway layouts. However, the results were not usually very satisfactory because of several problems which can arise, the most fundamental of which is the difference in purpose, and thus in design, of a poster and a model backscene, and this brings us to a very important principle in the design of a scenic background. A poster is intended to catch the eye amongst distracting surroundings, so its colour and composition will be as striking as possible. It will

Docks and harbours are interesting and attractive in model form. If based on a suitable small prototype, they need not occupy much space on a model railway but will add much both scenically and operationally. The scene shown here is part of a 6 ft by 4 ft 00 scale layout.

The smaller size of N scale allows a more elaborate dock to be featured. Graham Bailey built this interesting harbour scene complete with wharf, cranes, oil depot and shipbuilding yard for his medium–sized N scale layout. Both the oil tanker and the ship under construction were made up from Novo 'Shell Welder' plastic ship model kits.

Left *This large gravel hopper constructed from a Kibri HO scale kit is one of several realistic industrial structures available from Continental manufacturers which are also suitable for use on British prototype layouts. The picture is completed by the backscene, one of a range from the American firm Walthers.*

Below left *This facility for transferring rock products from rail to canal barge occupies little space but adds interest to the layout. The 4mm scale model was largely scratchbuilt but some plastic kit parts were used for convenience. It was modelled from a photograph of a coal staithe on the Aire & Calder Navigation Canal.*

Above right *This 4mm scale scrap-yard was based on a prototype yard near the Tyne river in Newcastle. Such an industry is ideal for a model railway layout as it provides not only scenic interest but also a siding for shunting, yet requires little space. Note the weathered crane and wagon.*

Right *Robert Tivendale's 4mm scale 'Wheal Louise' layout features a mineral railway serving a typical tin mine and treatment works. Careful research and accurate modelling has resulted in an authentic and interesting model. This picture shows the treatment works section of the layout. The locomotive in the foreground is a scratchbuilt model of* Miner, *an 0-6-0T built for the Redruth and Chasewater Railway in 1854 by Neilson and Co of Glasgow as an 0-4-0 and rebuilt into an 0-6-0 at Devoran in 1869 (Len Weal).*

Two scenes on Howard Coulson's 'Eitomo', an 009 layout based on the East African narrow gauge railways. The choice of an overseas prototype can be an interesting challenge and lead to the creation of a very different layout with great appeal.

Alan Copas created a very effective backscene for his N scale 'Fort Ness' layout by combining calendar and other pictures.

also be a complete and balanced picture in itself. The purpose of a scenic background is, however, quite different. We do not want it to draw the viewer's attention away from the modelled landscape; it should merely enhance and frame the layout. As the observer's gaze reaches the limit of the modelled landscape he should become aware of the scene apparently extending away into the distance but ideally there should be little or nothing on the backdrop to attract attention away from the modelled scenery, structures and trains. This principle applies whatever form of backscene is employed, and must be a guide whenever designing a background.

Another problem which arises with posters is that, if they are to be joined, matching may be difficult, particularly if they are different in artistic style, the use of colour, scale and so on. In fact, calendar pictures and colour pictures from magazines, particularly covers, are the best source of material for this method of producing backscenes. Catalogues for plastic structure kits often have colour pictures of completed models which can be cut out and employed as 'flats' or added to other backscenes to give variety. With these calendar and other colour pictures the most successful approach is to cut out and rearrange the features from the pictures to produce the effect you want. Care and thought is needed in the selection and arrangement for the best results, but the method can be very successful so take time moving the pictures around in various ways before deciding on the most suitable. Modelled or low-relief features can be used to mask joins where these would be obvious or obtrusive.

Another method which may appeal particularly to the photo enthusiast is the use of a photomural (a large photographic enlargement) as a backscene. This should preferably be either a colour

mural or a tinted black and white print. Photographic backgrounds are particularly effective when the scene on the layout is itself to be photographed; if properly arranged, a photographic background can then be indistinguishable from the real scene. A problem here is, of course, cost, especially if the modeller does not have the facilities or expertise to do the photographic work himself and must have it done professionally. Colour murals are particularly expensive.

Rather than use actual enlargements, we can utilize photography as a guide to painting a backscene. Suitable slides can

A photographic enlargement forms the backscene for this diorama featuring a coaling stage and water tower built from kits produced by the American manufacturer, Campbell Scale Models. Note how the fence has been used to conceal the join between the modelled scenery and the backdrop (Campbell Scale Models).

Neat modelling on the Milton Model Railway Group 7mm scale 'Woolbridge' layout is enhanced by the painted backscene giving a very realistic overall effect. The photograph was taken at an exhibition and shows that special lighting is not necessary for model photography provided the available illumination is even.

be projected on to the paper and the required features sketched in; parts of different slides can, of course, be combined as desired. Then the backdrop is painted, referring to the transparencies as a guide for the colours.

This leads us on to the backscene drawn and painted by the modeller to suit his specific requirements. You may feel that artistic ability and training would be essential if you are to produce a convincing drawn and painted scenic background, and, while it is obviously helpful to have some artistic skill and experience, most modellers should be able to make a reasonably effective and realistic backscene if they keep to a few

basic rules and do not try to be too ambitious.

One of the most important of these rules is to keep the picture simple, which, happily, makes our task much easier. In distant scenes, most of the small details are too far away to be visible, so to achieve the required illusion of distance on the backscene, we want a broad general impression rather than a picture with many small details. Indeed, too many features in a scenic background, particularly if they are clear and sharply defined, will make the background seem close, whereas a relatively empty scene with the outlines tending to be a little hazy and ill-defined will give an impression of greater spaciousness and distance. Not only should we depict relatively few features in the scene, but those chosen should be simple and will, therefore, be easier to represent realistically. Fields, hills, mountains, trees, bushes, hedges and other natural features are easier to show than rivers, roads and other man-made items. Structures can be particularly difficult because of problems with perspective; anything drawn in perspective on the backscene will only look right if viewed from one position, or at least from a point fairly close to this ideal viewpoint. If you do want to portray buildings on the scenic background, the difficulty can be minimized by depicting the structures as far in the distance as possible, and by showing one side of any building square on rather than drawing it so that two sides have to be seen in perspective.

The illusion of distance is created not only by the small size of the painted features on the backscene but also by the use of atmospheric perspective. The haze in the atmosphere causes the colours of distant objects to be muted and greyed. Thus, by choosing 'cool' colours, greens, blues and purples, the background will seem to recede. Avoid 'warm' colours such as red and orange because these brighter tones will have the opposite effect. The more distant an object is, the greyer its colour will seem, so as fields, hills, trees and other features are added to the backscene, increasing amounts of white or grey should be added to the other colours as we work into the 'distance'. Sometimes, the addition of a little blue or purple as well can be very effective for the far distance.

Poster colours are probably the easiest

A simple but very effective scene on the Southampton MRS 'Overcombe' 4mm scale layout. The backscene is hand-painted and gives a good impression of distance. Note the three birds in flight to the left of the river in the foreground.

for the beginner to use. Start by mounting plain white poster paper on hardboard sheeting using waterproof glue. When dry, sketch in the features of the background scene; use photographs, pictures, projected slides or even commercial backdrops as a guide if you wish, but do not try to copy exactly. Then paint the scene, remembering that a broad general impression is what is required and that it does not matter if the outlines are a little indefinite. Grass tends to be more yellow than one thinks, so we need a yellowy green rather than a blue green; it is usually necessary to add some yellow to the green poster paint before use. Paint trees and bushes as blobs of green paint merging together to form the mass of the tree or bush. Make the blobs lighter on top and darker below to represent the effects of light and shade and thus give shape and form. The sky can be painted cobalt blue with white added, the amount of white being steadily increased as we work from the top downwards so that the sky becomes almost white just above the horizon. Clouds require practice for realistic results so are perhaps best omitted at first.

Many modellers choose to use commercially produced backscenes. Though the approach is not as individual as creating your own scenic background, there are advantages. They have been specially designed for the purpose so that the choice of subject, the scale and the colouring are all appropriate. Often the perspective has been drawn so that the scenes are realistic from a reasonable range of viewpoints rather than from only one very limited position. Most are printed in full colour from artist's drawings except for the Faller and Vollmer sheets which appear to be reproductions of colour photographs. The manufacturers usually design their backgrounds so that different sheets from the set can be fitted together in any order with the joins matching realistically. It is also often possible to combine sheets or parts of sheets from different manufacturers successfully; trees, buildings or other features can be employed to cover the joins as necessary. However, variations in styles and colours may cause difficulties in some cases.

Modellers are now fortunate in having a really very good range of background scenes, both in scope and in quality, on the market from manufacturers in Britain, the United States, Germany and Switzerland. Naturally, the British designed and produced scenes are the most appropriate for layouts set in this country, though some of the others are also suitable. We must, of course, match up as far as possible the type of scene shown on the backdrop with the modelled scenery and structures. It is usually possible to find a scene from the range available that is suitable though this is a limitation to the employment of these commercially produced backgrounds. Another disadvantage is the loss of individuality on a layout because the same scenes appear so often on other model railways. However, despite these potential drawbacks, the commercial backscenes do have much to recommend them. They are generally well designed and produced, they are reasonably priced and they make it easy to complete the scenic landscape in a realistic way.

Because they come ready-made, it can be easy to consider them merely as a form of instant background scenery which requires little effort on our part to install. However, with a little more thought and work we can overcome the disadvantages mentioned above and achieve the most realistic results possible from these backscenes.

If the background is merely chosen and added after the rest of the scenery has been modelled, we are unlikely to end up with a really good match. It is therefore very important to consider which scenic background sheets we will want to use when we first start to plan the scenery; we should think of the modelled scenery and the background together as a single entity. Indeed, the best results may well come from choosing and erecting suitable backscenes as the first step in planning and modelling the scenery. After the background is in place, the three-dimensional landscape can be modelled using the printed scenery of the backdrop as a guide for the contours and colours of the foreground. This approach will help to unify the two with a more realistic overall appearance.

A criticism of the commercially produced scenes is that their familiarity from being seen so frequently on layouts detracts from their effectiveness. One way to disguise this sameness is to create a montage made up of sections cut from one or more scenic backgrounds mounted together. This will alter the appearance and give an original look to the composite backscene, and some of the manufacturers have designed their products to facilitate this. One of the Peco sheets consists of features specifically intended for cutting out and mounting on other sheets in the series to provide extra variety. The Townscene backgrounds produced by Brian Sherriff Ltd also include many separate and complete buildings to be cut out and

assembled in any order or combination, making this series very versatile indeed. Rather than having a sky background on each sheet, which would make it difficult to conceal the joins between the sheets, this firm markets sky backgrounds 11 yards long in a roll; the modeller can then cut whatever length he needs in one piece with no joins, and the various buildings can be mounted on it as required to create a complete backscene. The Swiss-made backgrounds by MZZ of Zurich, and available in Britain from Swiss Trains of Aberdeen, are also flexible in design allowing many variations to suit the individual modeller. Though based on Swiss structures and scenery, many of the sheets are also very suitable for British prototype layouts, and many of the structures featured can be built as flats or as low-relief models.

In addition to the sheets designed by the manufacturers to be used for montage or collage effects, there is, of course, no reason why you should not treat the ordinary sheets in a similar manner giving even greater scope for variation. The sheets employed can all be from the same manufacturer or you can even combine features from the products of different makers.

An alternative to mounting these added features directly on to the backscene is to make them into 'flats' or cut-outs, as with stage scenery in theatres. The cut-out features can be mounted on thick card or thin plywood and positioned a centimetre or two in front of the background. If you wish, there can even be two or three rows of these flats each slightly separated from the one behind to give an effect of depth. The card or plywood should be sanded to thin the edges which can then be touched up

Above *An effective combination of low-relief structures and a composite backscene gives a big city atmosphere to this scene on Bernard Taylor's N scale 'Bridgenshaw' layout. The hoardings and low-relief buildings are placed to conceal the join of modelled and flat scenery. Note also the weathering on the oil tankers (Len Weal).*

Below *Low-relief structures and a hand-painted backscene create a realistic town setting for Shepton Gurney station on Robert Petch's 00 gauge layout.*

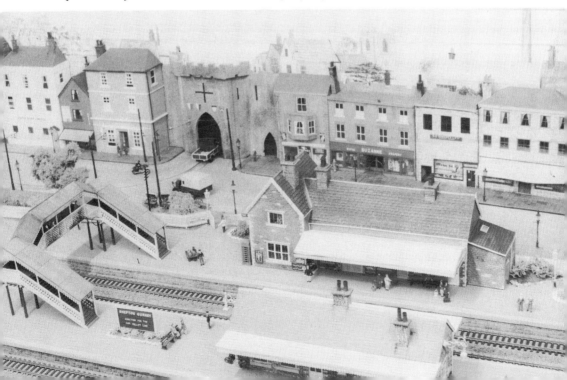

with paint to match the printed features. The back of each flat should be painted with matt black paint. The appearance of these flats can be enhanced by adding a little relief or texture to them. For example, scenic dressing or sawdust of an appropriate colour can be sprinkled over glue to add texture, and small pieces of lichen can be added to represent bushes. Buildings featured as cut-outs can be improved by adding relief with details such as window-sills, doorsteps, drain-pipes, door-knobs, projecting brickwork and so on. Windows can be cut out and clear plastic glazing added; black card fitted behind will prevent the viewer from seeing that there is no depth to the building.

Partly concealing the backscene with modelled features, either in full or low-relief, will make it less obvious. Town scenes in particular can be very effective with a combination of low-relief structures, buildings flats and a printed scenic background; try various arrangements to decide which will be the most realistic before finally fixing all the different features in position. A very attractive night effect can be achieved by making small holes where there are windows in some of the buildings on the scenic background and fitting small lights behind the backscene. Similarly, flats and low-relief structures can have small bulbs fitted behind them.

The treatment of the join between the modelled scenery and the flat printed backscene is very important in achieving a realistic result. We want them to blend imperceptibly and so we must disguise or conceal the actual join. One method is to mask the join with modelled features, either in full or low-relief, such as trees, bushes, low hills, an embankment or structures. Appropriate placing of a wall or fence is an effective method and one

which requires a minimum of space, and a slight gap left between the modelled and printed scenery will give a greater effect of depth. For example, at the rear of the layout we may have a grassy bank with a fence or hedge along the top. If the back of this bank drops straight down 1 or 2 centimetres in front of the scenic background, it will realistically conceal the join. If we are using a backdrop which includes structures, we can erect a fence or wall just in front of the backscene. The flat cut-outs mentioned earlier and low-relief buildings can also be employed very successfully to screen the join between the modelled and printed scenery from the viewer's eye. Whatever method is used, it is essential that the lighting for the layout is arranged so that none of the modelled, low-relief or cut-out features can cast any shadows on to the scenic background, as this will be very noticeable and will spoil any illusion of a distant scene.

Another technique for dealing with the join is to carry the modelled scenery right up to the scenic background and merge the two. This is simplest if the background is merely sky and the modelled landscape features a bank or low hills at the rear. However, it has also been very effectively applied to mountain scenery by blending the modelled and printed or painted scenery. The modelled plaster scenery surface is brought part way up the mountains shown on the backdrop and is textured and painted to match the colours of the scene making the colours greyer and bluer towards the rear of the scene to give the effect of distance and to match the backscene. Trees and bushes can be a mixture of fully modelled items, some that are partly modelled and stuck on to the printed scene and the ones already

On the 'Burnhopedale' 009 layout built by the Middlesbrough Model Railway and Tramway Club, the modelled scenery is carried up on to the painted backscene at the rear of the layout, and gives a most realistic effect.

on the background or added to it by being painted on. By using smaller and smaller trees as we go further towards the rear of the modelled scenery, we can create forced perspective and give a greater feeling of depth and distance.

This method of using smaller models towards the rear of a layout can also be applied to model buildings. For example, on an 00 scale layout buildings to go at the back of the layout can be modelled in 3mm scale or even in N scale to give exaggerated perspective and an impression of greater scenic depth.

CHAPTER 11
Figures

Human and animal figures make up a very important part of the model railway scene, and there has been a considerable change in attitudes towards the inclusion of miniature figures on model railway layouts in recent years. At one time, their use was not favoured, one of the arguments against their employment being that it was not realistic to have static models of 'living' people, and as they could not be made to move naturally they were better omitted altogether. Admittedly, the figures available at that time were rather crudely modelled, often considerably out of scale and usually unrealistically gloss painted. If employed at all, they were limited to a few railway staff and passengers waiting on the station platform. More recently, under the influence of imaginative modellers such as the late John Allen, and with the availability of well-proportioned and detailed figures, true to scale and in natural postures, they have become an imporant feature of model railway scenes. Indeed, on some layouts hundreds of figures have been included.

This is a much more logical approach. After all, the railway, the real railway, was built to serve the needs of the people, carrying them on passenger trains and transporting their goods and products on freight services. People also build, maintain and run the railway. Thus we need to have model figures very much in evidence on a layout to justify the presence of the railway and to emphasize its purpose.

Most modellers expect to put a good deal of time and effort into making their trains, structures and scenery realistic but often give little thought to selecting and placing figures to their best advantage. We should perhaps first of all consider what benefits we can hope to achieve with the effective use of these human and animal figures. There are various ways in which they can help to create the scenic setting we want. They help to give a sense of scale to the layout by providing something of a size known to everyone who views the model railway, even if they are not railway enthusiasts, and to which other features can be related. They identify the type of activity taking place by their positions, postures and clothing, and they also help to establish the period in which the layout is supposed to be set. They are also very effective in directing the eye of the viewer; figures tend to attract attention and thus draw the viewer's gaze to

wherever you wish. They also add interest and help to inform the viewer
about the scene, especially when they
are grouped to tell a little story about
what is happening. Because they can
contribute so significantly to the overall
realism of the layout, we must get away
from the old idea of thinking of them as
unimportant and merely to be dumped
down anywhere convenient. Indeed, a

Numerous figures have been included in this scene on Dave Rowe's 'Axford' layout to give the impression of a busy market day in the town. The buildings are from Honiton and Sidmouth while the arches in the foreground are from Exeter. Superb modelling of carefully selected prototypes and their arrangement in a natural and harmonious grouping has created a fictitious town which looks real (Brian Monaghan).

relatively ordinary scene can be completely transformed by the imaginative use of figures.

We are fortunate today in the wide range of good quality commercially-produced model figures. Examples are available for all the popular railway scales, either as models intended for railway use or as figures which can be converted from military or other models. In 00 and H0 scales, a very large range of figures for railway workers, civilians and soldiers is available. With a little care, the modeller working in 00 scale can usually employ H0 scale as well as 00 scale figures, even though the former will be rather on the small side. After all, real people also vary quite a lot in size! The Preiser H0 scale range is

especially extensive, including a very wide range of occupations and activities and the modelling is excellent. Both these and the Merten range, also H0 scale, are hard plastic figures sold ready-painted in small sets; they are, however, quite expensive, especially as most layouts need large numbers. Many of the Preiser figures are also marketed as unpainted selections of 120 or so figures, which are of course much cheaper per figure and represent very good value. British 00 scale plastic figures, painted and unpainted, are made by various manufacturers including Dapol, Merit and Slater, but the range is limited. Many hard plastic military figures are also available and are often suitable for conversion for use on model railway

A typical country hotel, the 'Ship Inn', realistically modelled in 4mm scale by Mike Gill. The visitors arriving by charabanc add life and interest to the scene (Mike Gill).

taking time and care for the best possible results. You may feel that figures of this size are too small for detail painting but this is not so, as will be evident from looking at the work of military modellers in this scale.

Matt paints are required for figure painting and the Humbrol range is very suitable. You will also need thinners and small disposable dishes for mixing; I find foil milk-bottle tops convenient as they are a handy size, easily obtained and cost nothing. You should also use good quality brushes; some modellers like to use very fine brushes, while others prefer to work with small, rather than very small, brushes as they tend to keep a fine point better and this is the most important feature when painting fine details. It is essential to take good care of your brushes — they should be cleaned with thinners or brush cleaner immediately after use, then washed in warm water with a little detergent added and finally the point should be shaped with your fingers and the brush stored upright with the head uppermost.

The paint should be thoroughly stirred before use. Failure to do this may result in the colour not being exactly right and the paint drying shiny rather than matt. In common with the practice of painting models generally, and as discussed more fully in the chapter on weathering, it is a good idea to add a few drops of white to your basic colour.

There are some general principles worth following when painting figures. Whenever possible it is best to paint the light-coloured areas first. Then, if any of the paint you are applying spreads over the edges of this area it will be easily covered when you come to paint the adjacent darker areas. If, conversely, you paint the darker areas first, any of the

darker paint which spreads beyond the borders will be more difficult to cover and may show through the paler colour when it is applied. It is usually most convenient to start by painting the face and hands, using Humbrol Flesh. Then work outwards from the inner layers of clothing; shirt and trousers to coat and shoes. It is convenient and time-saving to paint several figures at the same time, especially if they are wearing clothes of similar colours. You may also find it helpful to use a magnifier, either one of the self-standing types which leave both hands free or alternatively the magnifying goggles that you can wear. It is also a good idea to provide yourself with a support against which you can steady your hand as you carry out the fine detail painting.

If this basic painting is neatly carried out, the models will already look quite effective. However, the appearance will be greatly enhanced by appropriate shading which will give realistic form and shape to the face and clothing. This is because the relief on these tiny figures, though correctly modelled, is insufficient to cast the shadows which create the effect of the depth and roundness of real faces and clothing. Adding highlights and shadows compensates for this and greatly enhances the realism. You may not want to do this for all your figures, but for those in the foreground it is worth while, particularly as it is easier to do than you might think. For the face, add a little red-brown to the basic flesh colour, thinning as necessary. Use this to shade the eye sockets, under the nose and beneath the jaw, and to paint in the mouth. Then lighten the basic flesh tone with a little white and use this to highlight the forehead, nose and cheeks, blending them into the basic flesh col-

Shading and highlighting faces and clothing on model figures gives a realistic effect as can be seen with this railway worker standing outside the freight depot on Paul Stapleton's narrow gauge 'Yakima Valley' layout. The firewood, sacks, barrels and other small details also add interest to the scene (Len Weal).

our. Once the face is dry, add a dot of black for the iris of each eye and paint in the eyebrows and hair. Hands are painted with the darkened flesh tone and then dry brushed with the lighter colour to give highlights on the fingers.

For the clothes the principle is similar. Folds and creases are shaded with a little of the basic colour darkened with a trace of black; this is also used to paint the cuffs and lapels. Then use the basic colour lightened with a little white to highlight the tops of folds, the shoulders and the top of the hat, if one is worn. This highlighting can be done very effectively with a dry-brush technique; dip the brush lightly into the colour, wipe most of the paint off and then brush gently over the areas to be highlighted.

While the results of the painting may appear rather crude through the magnifier, they will look very effective at normal viewing distances. Remember that we have deliberately exaggerated the shading and highlighting to make them visible at a distance, much as is done with stage make-up.

In addition to the selection of plastic figures, mainly from Continental makers, there is also a range of cast metal figures from British manufacturers such as Langley, Scalelink, Ratio, Dart and Springfield. Similar modifications and improvements can be made to these metal figures as described above for the plastic models, but using epoxy

Careful painting will give features a lifelike appearance which will enhance the realism of a model railway as in this scene at Sweetwater station on Paul Stapleton's On2½ 'Yakima Valley' layout based on American prototype narrow gauge railroading. Note also the bird sitting on the roof of the station building (Len Weal).

adhesives and fillers. After a coat of metal primer, painting can be carried out in the same way as for the plastic figures.

While the quality of the figures themselves and the standard of the painting are obviously important in achieving realism, care must also be taken in the way in which they are positioned on the layout. Mount the figures with a spot of adhesive beneath each foot. Alternatively, if the positioning may be only temporary, for example for photography or while trying out various groupings, the figures can be held in place with tiny blobs of Blu-Tack beneath the feet. Make sure the figures are in natural poses, it is all too easy to mount them so that they lean over in positions that no real person

could ever maintain! In general, it also looks rather unnatural to have model figures posed as though in motion; they appear more realistic if they are between movements. For example, it will look better to have a workman pausing and leaning on his pick rather than in mid swing. The exception to this general rule is in the creation of scenes for model photography. We are used to seeing pictures in which the camera has stopped everyone in mid action, so it also appears quite natural in model photographs. Indeed, it can make them more realistic and interesting because it gives them more apparent life and activity.

The placing and grouping of model figures is also important; try out various

This ploughing scene adds interest to the lineside on Bruce Wilson's 'Wakeley Keyne' 4mm scale 9mm gauge (009) layout. Note the seagulls following the farmer and his plough and also the workmen repairing the fence and the shepherd at the rear of the layout. The photograph was taken using the light available at an exhibition.

positionings to create natural looking groups. Certain groupings of figures will encourage the viewer's eye to be drawn to areas with special interest or extra detailing. For example, figures may be grouped around a wagon, locomotive or road vehicle, outside a building or beside some repair work, and will draw attention to the feature concerned.

In addition to appearing more realistic and natural, grouping the figures will also make them seem more numerous than if they were spread evenly over the layout. Crowd scenes can be very effective, and some fine examples can be seen in the Preiser catalogue.

There is also a good selection of animal figures on the market, particularly in 00 and H0 scales. Wild animals, large and small, farm stock, circus animals and even domestic pets are included ranging from elephants to rabbits, cats and various breeds of dog. There is even a good variety of birds in plastic and cast metal, at least in 00 and H0 scales, with pigeons, seagulls, swans, ducks, geese and even an eagle. I have also seen some very realistic swans and seagulls scratch-built from scraps of wood and card, and with fine wire sup-

A scene on the 7mm scale 16.5mm Talyllyn Country layout built by Robert Hailes. The natural poses and positioning of the railway worker figures add to the realism.

ports we can even model birds in flight very effectively.

The same principles in preparing the models and painting them apply as for the human figures, and in the same way it is possible to make modifications as re-quired. As with humans, aim for natural groupings of the animals on your layout, for example a herd of cows on the way to the milking shed, or a flock of sheep with a shepherd and his dogs.

CHAPTER 12
A snow scene

Model railway layouts show a remarkable variety in choice of prototype, location and period, as well as in the style of presentation, reflecting the very diverse interests of enthusiasts. However, in one respect they are all surprisingly similar; almost all layouts are set in the summer season, with bright blue skies, green trees, flowers in bloom and with the model inhabitants dressed in lightweight clothes, or even sunbathing or swimming. Very rarely do we find a layout set in winter. This is understandable, as for many modellers a fine hot summer day is the ideal, and there is a strong nostalgic appeal about the days of summers past, always remembered as hotter and longer than at the present. However, it is rather a pity that winter is neglected by most railway modellers. A glance at the prototype or pictures of it in snowy conditions will show just how attractive and interesting such a scene can be. In the same way, a winter setting for a model railway can be very effective, the more so because it is so rarely represented on a layout. The relative starkness of the snowy setting makes the trains and other railway features stand out to especially good effect, and more strikingly than against the normal green of the summer landscape.

While you may not wish to model a whole layout with a wintry setting, the inclusion of one snow-covered area is certainly well worth considering. One way in which this can be done is to model part of the layout, perhaps a section served by a branch line, as a mountainous area with a covering of snow — this has been accomplished very effectively on layouts based on American, Swiss and German prototypes. An interesting modern layout design scheme is to have two or even three levels, one above the other, on an along-the-wall layout, enabling a much more extensive layout to be created in the space available, and spirals of track, partly or wholly concealed in tunnels, may be employed to link the different levels. The visual separation thus introduced means that quite different scenic settings can be modelled without compromising the realism. A mountainous snowy area can be convincingly modelled on the upper level of such a layout, enhancing the illusion of high altitude.

Another modern idea in layout design is the separation of the layout into two or more parts by complete scenic breaks.

Len Weal created this snow scene as a diorama for photographic purposes. The smoke is teased out cotton wool (Len Weal).

Using this type of scheme, one part of the layout could be modelled as in winter and another as in summer without spoiling the realism.

As always, if you decide to model a snow scene observation of the real thing or study of suitable photographs is essential to achieve a realistic effect. Look at the shape and form of the snow-covered landscape, the way drifts have formed, how snow covers structures, trees, fences and other features, where icicles form and their appearance. Once we know the sort of effect we are hoping to create, we must find a suitable material to represent the snow; we need a white substance with the right texture and, if possible, also the sparkle of snow. Many different substances have been employed, particularly for temporary scenes set up for photographic purposes. These include flour, salt, baking soda, plaster, Polyfilla, scouring powder, sugar and talcum powder. Of these, salt is particularly suitable as it has a realistic sparkle, but its use is only feasible for temporary scenes and it must not be allowed to get damp as it will then become sticky and difficult to clean up. For a permanent snow scene, plaster or Polyfilla is most suitable.

If the snow cover is to be complete, we need only to model the basic contours as far as the bare white shape using Mod-Roc plaster bandage material or some other basic scenery foundation. No ground cover or texture material is required, and over this basic shape the

A fall of snow transforms the prototype scene and the results can be very attractive. This photograph was taken in mid-winter in Uppsala in Sweden, and modelling snow scenes on your layout can be very rewarding.

plaster or filler is applied. Spray the plaster with water using one of the simple sprayers now available for watering houseplants, then shape and smooth it with wet fingers or a wet brush to give the desired contours of fallen or drifted snow. Sprinkle on a little more plaster or filler and then spray gently again with water. Leave the surface to set hard and then paint it, using matt white emulsion brushed on to cover the whole surface. Dave Frary, an expert scenic modeller from America, has developed, after much experimentation with various materials, a 'snow' mix which is very effective in appearance and which forms a hard semi-gloss surface which is easy to clean. He mixes equal quantities of Acrylic Matte Medium, Acrylic Modelling Paste and Titanium White artist's tube acrylic paint and applies the mixture with a brush; this is an excellent alternative to the white emulsion paint finish. Over either of these snow surfaces a thin wash of blue should be applied to give form to the snowbanks and drifts by creating shadows and hollows. Some modellers have used white and terest to the scene.

You may prefer to model a light coating of snow rather than a deep snowfall. In that case you will need to colour the scenery in the normal way, using mainly greys and browns for the winter landscape. Grass and weeds can be modelled from string or carpet fibres, also coloured with browns and greys. Add bushes of lichen and trees, either evergreens or bare-branched deciduous varieties. A light covering of snow can be represented very effectively by the use of an aerosol can of matt white paint, or with an airbrush. Spray from a distance in one direction only, applying lightly so that only a partial covering results, and taking care to avoid a spotty effect. Alternatively, a light sprinkling of plaster could be used to achieve a similar appearance. White paint is then dry-brushed on to fallen logs, rocks and other surfaces to represent collected snow.

To complete the snow scene, white paint can be applied to the scenery shown on the scenic background, thus carrying the effect into the distance. A final touch is appropriate lighting for the scene. A diffuse white light gives a good effect and a small light with a blue filter can give just a touch of blueness in the shadows making the scene appear even more wintry.

A disadvantage in modelling a permanent snow scene is that the white surfaces tend to show the dust and dirt more quickly and noticeably than other scenes and so more care is required with regular cleaning. It will also be necessary to repaint the scene from time to time.

To conclude, I would like to mention two other methods of representing snow which may appeal to some readers. The West German firm of Faller, well known for their model structure kits in plastic and in plastic and card combined, now offer a kit for modelling snow scenes with a snow mix that can be applied to buildings and trees to give a realistic winter effect. Another material which can be employed is the spray-on snow marketed around Christmas-time which is sold for the purpose of making Christmas decorations but can also be used for creating model snow scenes.

CHAPTER 13
Model railway photography

The photography of models in general and of model railways in particular has become increasingly popular in recent years, and this trend has been reflected by a noticeable improvement in the standard of photographs appearing in the model press. Suitable photographic equipment of good quality is now available at a reasonable price and many enthusiasts find that photographing their models adds enjoyment and satisfaction to the hobby. Having spent many hours building a model it is very rewarding to

be able to depict it in an interesting and realistic photograph.

Now you may feel that this is all very well but that a section on photographing your models and layouts is a digression from my chosen theme of adding realism to your model railway. However, I would argue that it is relevant for at least two good reasons. Photography is a very revealing way of checking your models for faults and flaws. When we look at a model, particularly one we ourselves have built, it is very easy to see it subjec-

A low camera angle gives a realistic view of Alistair, *a 2-6-2 Manning Wardle tank locomotive, on P.D. Hancock's famous 4mm scale narrow gauge 'Craig & Mertonford Railway'* (P.D. Hancock).

tively as we expect it to be and as we imagined the finished model would look while we were building it. We are thus very prone to overlook minor faults or errors in construction and finish which can detract from its realism. The camera, on the other hand, is objective and records exactly what is there, and any defects are much more noticeable in a photograph. Close study of the pictures will thus reveal anything which is not just right and appropriate corrections can be made. This also helps us to improve our modelling techniques in general and future models will benefit and be more realistic.

However, there is another reason which is perhaps even more important and which relates to the scenic setting and overall appearance of a model railway. Taking photographs of your layout will help you to develop an eye for good pictures with pleasing and realistic arrangements. The very principles of composition, form, balance and framing which are so important in photography are also relevant in scenic design, and the practice and experience gained from photography will help in creating interesting and realistic settings on the layout.

Many enthusiasts have been successful in model photography, and others whose experience is so far limited to family and holiday snaps would also like to try it. However, initial attempts can be disappointing. Model railway photography is not difficult but the techniques required are different from those needed in ordinary photography. Before looking at the equipment and techniques, we should consider what we are aiming for in taking good model pictures.

It is of course important that the sub-ject is in sharp focus so that it can be clearly seen. We want a well-composed picture with an arrangement that is pleasing to the eye and which directs attention towards the subject. Generally we want to choose a viewpoint which will make the model look as realistic as possible; a low angle often enhances this effect, and it is also usually a good principle to fill the photograph with the subject and to eliminate other features which are unnecessary or irrelevant to the picture.

The subject of photography generally is a complex one about which many books have been written. It is certainly not possible to cover the subject fully here, nor would it be relevant as we are concerned only with those aspects which relate specifically to model photography. I am assuming that you have, or can acquire from other books, at least some basic knowledge of photography and of how to use a camera, and I want merely to indicate the equipment and techniques that may be used. Those discussed are purely my personal preferences but they are simple and do seem to work satisfactorily, even under the rather difficult conditions which often prevail at exhibitions. However, they are certainly not the only way and other photographers may well prefer a different approach. What is important is to be very familiar with your camera and other equipment so that you can handle it easily and confidently, and also to establish a method of working which will consistently produce technically satisfactory pictures. You will then be free to concentrate your attention on the more artistic aspects of making interesting and realistic pictures while knowing that your basic technique will not let you down.

The basic equipment required for model railway photography is relatively modest; you can always add extra items later if you wish. By far the most suitable camera for our purposes is a 35mm single lens reflex camera. The studio camera with its tilts and swings and larger film sizes is a more versatile instrument which produces superb quality pictures, but it is more suited to the professional or advanced amateur than to the average enthusiast. The single lens reflex camera allows you to see through the viewfinder exactly what will appear on the negative and this is particularly important in close-up work. Most of these cameras also have interchangeable lenses and with the use of extension tubes between the lens and the camera body it is possible to focus close enough to photograph even very small models. Although you can pay a great deal for a camera of this type, they need not be expensive, and quite adequate models are available in the cheaper price ranges. A further economy can be made by buying second-hand; I have purchased most of my photographic equipment in this way including several cameras, lenses, exposure meter, tripod and an enlarger. You will often find second-hand equipment in very good condition on sale in photographic shops, and most detailers offer a 3 or 6 month guarantee on such items. Often the camera or other item has been used very little and appears virtually new. Provided you keep clear of obviously worn or badly-treated equipment, you should have no problems and the savings can be considerable.

In general, a basic camera which you can handle easily may well be better for the purpose than a more expensive one which has lots of extras which you do not really need and which may make the camera more complicated to use. The standard 50mm or 55mm focal length lens fitted to these 35mm cameras is perfectly satisfactory for model photography and is the easiest lens to learn to use. An f3.5 lens is all that is needed, though most SLR cameras these days are sold with an even better f2.8 or f2 lens; a large aperture is not really necessary for our purposes as most of the pictures will be taken with the lens stopped right down to the smallest aperture of f16 or f22 for maximum depth of field.

Depth of field is much more of a problem in taking model pictures than in ordinary photography because it is very limited in close-up work. The depth of field is the extent of the scene, from front to back, which is in sharp focus, and it depends on three factors. The shorter the distance from the lens to the subject, the less the depth of field, and it is thus relatively shallow in model photography. Secondly the smaller the aperture, the greater the depth of field, so for model work we should almost always use the lens at the smallest aperture (highest f number) of the lens; this is usually f16 or f22, but sometimes f32. The third factor is the focal length of the lens; the shorter this is, the greater the depth of field. To some extent, this advantage is countered by the fact that with a shorter focal length (wide angle) lens one must move closer to the subject to maintain the same image size on the negative. However, overall we do gain depth of field by moving in closer with a wide angle lens. This also gives a realistic effect because the camera is more within the scene at a nearer to scale distance from the subject, so wide angle lenses are quite popular for model photography. It is important not to tilt the

This page and overleaf *It is often possible to frame your model railway photographs with various features thus directing the viewer's eye to the subject and adding to the effectiveness of the picture.* **Above** *A tunnel mouth has been used to frame the locomotive and its train in this eye level view.* **Right** *A scene on Graham Lindley's 009 'Lydd Valley' layout. Framing the picture with part of a span and pier of a viaduct leads the eye of the viewer to the subject, a model of a County Donegal railcar.*

Left *An arch of a high railway viaduct frames this view of a rural scene modelled in 4mm scale by Terry Jenkins.*

Below *Tree branches in both upper corners of this photograph help to keep the viewer's attention on the locomotive. The scene is on the H0 scale metre gauge Swiss prototype layout built by Mike and David Polglaze.*

camera as this will lead to distortion problems which are particularly marked with short focal length lenses. The 28mm focal length lenses are the most suitable wide angle lenses for this type of photography; long focal length lenses (telephoto and long zoom lenses) are rarely useful for model railway photography.

Because we will be using the camera with the lens stopped right down to give maximum depth of field, long exposures will be required for enough light to reach the film; thus a tripod is essential. This should be sturdy enough to avoid any camera shake but not so heavy or bulky that you cannot carry it conveniently. A cable release is also a good idea so that exposures can be made without any risk of inadvertently moving the camera.

Many SLR cameras have through-the-lens (TTL) metering and this has the advantage of automatically allowing for special situations, such as the increased exposure required for close-up pictures using extension tubes. However, I like to use a hand-held meter as well, as this enables me to check more easily that the lighting intensity is even throughout the scene.

For black and white work, a film with fine grain such as Kodak Panatomic X or Ilford FP4 is most suitable. There is no advantage in using a fast film as the grain is more marked and, since the subject is static there is no need for the higher film speed. For colour pictures I use Kodak (Ektachrome for artificial illumination and Kodachrome for daylight outdoors) or Fujichrome film.

The lighting arrangement is perhaps the single feature that causes most difficulty for the beginner. A sign of a successful set-up is that the lighting is not unduly noticeable when you view the finished print; it appears natural and unobtrusive. There are three things to be avoided: uneven lighting, often with the foreground too bright and the background very dark; excessively contrasty lighting with very bright highlights and with no detail in the shadows; and double or multiple shadows from more than one light source. When you are setting up the scene, all these effects are much less apparent to the eye, which tends to make allowances, than to the camera which faithfully records what it sees. Take some trial shots and make any adjustments needed to eliminate these errors. The more complex the lighting arrangements become, the more likely you are to run into difficulties, so I would recommend that you use the simplest scheme that you find will give you good results and stick to it.

I use two basic schemes. The first is for small single models (or small groups of them) to be shown against a plain (usually white) background. A sheet of white paper is used as the background and this is curved so that no unsightly crease or join is visible; adhesive tape can be used to hold it in position as needed. With the lens wide open for the clearest view, focus on a point about one-third of the way back on the model; in this way, you make maximum use of the available depth of field when you close the lens down to its smallest aperture to take the picture. I usually position the set-up beneath the room light (a single bulb with the shade removed), which will act as a fill-in to soften the shadows cast by the main light. For the latter I use a 60 watt pearl bulb in an Anglepoise lamp close to the camera position. This type of lamp can be adjusted for position very easily and conveniently and the reflector

Above *This 4mm scale model goods shed built by Derek Purkis was photographed against a white paper background using the simple set-up described in the text.*

Below *Malcolm Carlsson created an attractive silhouette effect by backlighting his period locomotive and wagon models* (Malcolm Carlsson).

makes the source a flood rather than a spot lamp. A meter reading is taken from the model (not from the background) but a longer exposure is needed than that given by this reading, partly to allow for the greater exposure required for close-ups (though this is allowed for if you are using the through-the-lens metering system) and partly because it is needed to give good detail in the shadows (models are often rather dark in colour). I usually take two pictures, one with twice and the other with four times the exposure indicated by the meter reading. In other words, if the meter reading gives 2 seconds, expose at 4 and 8 seconds respectively in successive shots. This, with normal or slight under-development (to reduce contrast), gives a negative which will print well on normal contrast paper. For colour pictures, I replace the two bulbs with Phillips No 1 Photoflood bulbs; these get quite hot so should not be left on for any longer than necessary.

For similar photographs of larger single models, scenes on a layout and dioramas, I use the room lighting if suitable or, if this is inadequate, the adjustable lamp positioned higher and further away than for the single small models. I aim to have a single main light source (representing the sun) and a weaker supplementary source (or sources) which should not cast shadows of their own but which help illuminate their shadows cast by the main light so that detail there is not lost. Instead of using lamps, this fill-in light can be provided by sheets of white card positioned so as to reflect light into the shadows. Do not place your light(s) too close to the scene, especially if the scene is a fairly large one, as this will lead to uneven lighting with the parts nearest to the light

being better illuminated than the more distant areas. It is worth remembering too that in real scenes the distant areas are usually lighter, so when lighting model scenes make sure that the background areas are well illuminated. A little care and practice is needed with the lighting to get good results, but the time and effort involved will be well worth while and the whole thing will become easier and more predictable as you gain experience. As with the smaller set-up for single models, use the meter to give an exposure time but take one picture at double this and one at four times as well. For colour pictures, substitute Photoflood bulbs and take particular care to achieve even lighting. Use the meter to give an exposure time, but bracket this with times a little longer and a little shorter as well.

A good alternative method, if the model can be moved, is to take your pictures outdoors using sunlight. This natural lighting is very effective and, of course, the illumination will be even. It can still be helpful to use pieces of white card as reflectors to soften the shadows, as the light can be rather harsh in bright sunshine. Take care that it is not windy as this may cause movement in the scene during exposure, or may even cause damage to the models.

When photographing models, particularly scenes where there may be numerous features including human figures and small details, do not be tempted to rush things. Take your time selecting the best angles and arrangements for a good composition, and check carefully just before exposing that none of the models has been displaced, that no figures have fallen over, that all the railway models have all their wheels on the track and that there are no out-of-

Night scenes can be very effective on model railways. This picture of the terminus on the 'Ambledown Line' built by Les Andrews was taken in the normal way but with the layout street lamps switched on; the negative was then printed darker than usual to give the effect of a moonlit night scene.

scale objects such as curtains or furniture intruding into the background. Such flaws are easy to overlook when you are busy concentrating on lighting, exposure times and so on, but are very obvious in the resulting photographs. Once you are satisfied with a set-up, take plenty of pictures from various angles as film (for black and white anyway) is relatively cheap; it is easy to take a few extra shots while you have everything arranged, but not so convenient later. A small change in camera postition or angle may make quite a difference to the picture, and hav-

ing a selection from which to choose will give you more chance of getting a really good final photograph.

Once you have got used to taking photographs of your layout, you may like to try some special effects. Night scenes are easy, particularly in black and white. Take the picture as usual but with any model lighting, such as street lamps, interior lighting in structures, train lights and so on, switched on. The negatives are then printed with extra exposure to give darker prints and result is a very effective night scene.

Right *Smoke can be added to model railway photographs by wrapping cotton wool around a piece of wire with one end fitted into the locomotive chimney and moving the wire during a time exposure.*

Below *In this picture, the Airfix Class '31' diesel locomotive model was moved during a time exposure to give a blurring effect suggesting movement and speed.*

If you do your own printing, darkroom manipulation enables a variety of effects to be achieved. These two very different scenes are from the same basic negative of a locomotive and snowplough in the snow, in each case printed in combination with another negative. **Above** The other negative was of a white disc (to represent the full moon) on a black background, and the combination was printed to give a dark picture. **Below** The other negative was of a black background splattered with white paint to give the effect of snow falling, and the combination was printed to give a day-time effect.

This winter scene is a photo-montage combining a model scene (in front of the fence) with a view of the real landscape (the fence and beyond) creating realistic effect.

An impression of train movement can be created by taking a picture with the train moving during the exposure — the more movement, the greater the blur — but you may need to experiment to get the effect you want. A more difficult technique is to pan the camera with the train during the exposure; if correctly done this renders the rolling-stock sharp and clear with a streaked, blurred background giving an impression of a speeding train.

For the best results in black and white photography, it is preferable to do your own developing and printing. This will allow you to exercise close control over all the stages and to make any necessary alterations. It will also enable you to produce special effects by darkroom manipulation of the images; for example, a real background can be combined with your models by double printing the two negatives.

However, you may not want to get involved in developing and printing, and in any case taking the pictures is the main thing. It is well worth having a go at model railway photography; it will add interest to your modelling as well as produce a fine record of your layout.

CHAPTER 14
A 'different' prototype

The basic theme throughout this book has been the adding of realism, but I have also tried to emphasize the importance of making a model railway interesting. After all, there is not much satisfaction to be derived from a layout which, though realistic and accurate to the prototype, is uninteresting for you to view and operate. I have already discussed some of the component parts of a layout such as the structures, and have stressed the importance of appropriate selection and grouping of the buildings in creating an interesting and realistic appearance. Similar principles apply to other features of the layout.

The choice of the prototype railway you model is, of course, of even more basic importance. Once this decision is made, many aspects of your layout will, within certain limits, be decided. If, for example, you choose to model a Great Western Railway branch line, you will have to set your model geographically within the territory covered by the GWR with appropriate scenery. Your track layout should be generally in accordance with those employed by the company and the railway structures will need to be of the characteristic architectural style and materials, and so on. Thus this initial

choice is a very important one, and I have mentioned some of the possibilities already in the section on planning. It is a choice which depends very much upon the personal interests of each individual modeller, and one of the attractions of railway modelling as a hobby is the very wide choice it offers to the enthusiast not only with regard to different prototypes to model but also in the various approaches which can be followed in doing so. If you have a particular interest in a certain prototype and wish to create a realistic model based on it, your basic choice will be easy and you can move on to consider the details. If, however, your interest is less specific, you will be looking at the various options. Personally, I have to admit to a liking for model railways that are a little different from the usual; at an exhibition with a selection of layouts of a comparable standard of realism and detail, it is the one based on an unusual prototype or with a rather different approach that I tend to find the most interesting. If you feel as I do and have no particular prototype in mind, you might like to consider an alternative to the traditional British-style layout.

A narrow gauge line is one possibility, though this kind of layout is now quite

A scene on Mike Sharman's superb mixed gauge (broad, standard and narrow) Victorian period 4mm scale layout.

common. However, the choice of a lesser-known prototype as the basis could lead to a rather different and interesting model. Less common and potentially very interesting is a broad gauge model railway, particularly a period layout featuring the Brunel 7 ft gauge, for which some commercial parts in 4mm scale and an excellent book of plans for locomotives and rolling-stock are available. However, the Irish, Spanish, and Australian broad gauges have also been modelled and would also be interesting choices of prototype.

In fact, broad gauge aside, the many foreign railways provide a rich and varied choice for the modeller who would like to try something a little different from the usual British prototype layout. It is particularly appealing to be able to combine an enjoyable foreign holiday with collecting ideas and information for a model railway layout, and there is also a freshness and interest in a prototype which is relatively new to one.

For practical modelling purposes, it is perhaps useful to divide foreign railways into three broad categories. The first includes those countries for which the railway modeller has considerable commercial support with a wide range of ready-to-run models, kits, accessories and detailing items. These include the United States and some European countries such as Germany, France and

Howard Coulson spent 18 months in Kenya and has since built a narrow gauge layout based on East African Railways. His personal knowledge of the prototype and the information he collected has enabled him to build a model with a realistic atmosphere.

Switzerland. In the second group are the railways for which some manufactured models are available providing a basis on which the modeller will have to build by adapting, converting and scratch-building other equipment, structures and so on. In this category are other European countries such as Spain and Denmark, together with some more distant lands such as Australia and Japan.

When we come to the third group, countries not mentioned above, there is little if anything available commercially and the modeller is largely on his own.

Thus the modeller can select from a group appropriate to his skill and experience and to the time he wishes to spend on obtaining information and building from scratch. The amount of prototype information available and the ease of acquiring it tends to parallel the supply of commercial model products. Thus there is a great deal of reference material for the United States both in the model railroading magazines (the best-known being *Model Railroader* and *Railroad Model Craftsman*) and in prototype magazines and books, and these are of course in English. French, German and Swiss railways are also well covered in model and prototype magazines and books published in those countries; a working knowledge of French or German is therefore very helpful though it is surprising how far one can get with only school French or German, particularly as the material is often well illustrated! Some information is also available in English in books and magazines, and some of the British model railway magazines feature foreign railways quite often, for example *Scale Model Trains*. Of course, *Continental Modeller* is entirely given over to foreign railway modelling not just European but the whole world. *Euromodel Rail Review* is another British magazine which covers European railways and model railways exclusively.

A modern light railway such as the Tyne & Wear Metro (shown here) or the London Docklands Railway would be an unusual and interesting choice of prototype.

CHAPTER 15

Modelling an overseas prototype

by Giles Barnabe

Giles Barnabe has chosen an unusual prototype to model and his account of his experiences in researching and building his layout gives some idea of just what is involved in modelling a little known foreign prototype.

Introduction

These days many modellers take the opportunity afforded by the availability of German, French and Swiss models to indulge in a layout set beyond the English Channel. Some even follow Spanish practice, though news of these brave souls is seldom seen in the model press. So what sort of lunatic attempts a model of a Spanish narrow gauge railway, and in particular the Majorcan Railways?

For a start, my taste in railways is biased towards the rural ramblings of either narrow gauge or the most marginal of standard lines. Past layouts have included a fictional 4mm scale Colonel Stephens branch line set in West Sussex and an American 'short line' modelled with suitably adapted N gauge stock. After the latter, I felt like a return to narrow gauge and a larger scale. At about the same time there was a convenient gap in my professional life and I remembered that once, on a holiday in Majorca, I had caught a glimpse of some narrow gauge tracks vanishing down an alley in one of the larger towns. Accordingly I decided to investigate, and luckily obtained a late holiday booking in a resort in the northeast of the island.

The trip was a great success, as I discovered a 3 ft gauge railway system, albeit partly in the throes of conversion to metre gauge, but also with many miles of undisturbed abandoned tracks left for nature to reclaim. Situated off the tourist routes, it was possible to imagine local life as it had been twenty or more years ago, and indeed some parts of the line looked as if a train might still be expected. Only on some level crossings had the roadway's asphalt been extended to cover the rails giving an air of permanence to the closure.

The whole system has more than a few echoes of the Isle of Man and County Donegal Railways and was at one time very similar to the latter with an extended main line having several long branches, whose lesser traffic was given over to railcars nearly fifty years ago. However, the Ferrocarriles de Majorca, to give the line its full name, was always a

Above *Today, the FCdeM is an all diesel railcar operation. Here railcar 2004 waits to leave Palma for Inca in 1981* (Giles Barnabe).

Below *The steam era on the FCdeM was typified by this shot of Nasmyth Wilson-built 4-4-0T No27* Arta. *The railway had a large number of similar 4-4-0Ts and also several 4-6-0Ts of a generally similar outline* (L.G. Marshall).

fairly basic undertaking. Even today, as continuous welded rail and colour light signals are introduced, there is no point interlocking, the turnouts being worked as always by individual trackside levers. Indeed, until the present conversion there was no signalling at all, train movements presumably being advised by telephone.

In addition to the FCdeM, it was found that the island has another 3 ft gauge line. This links the capital, Palma, with the port of Soller on the north coast, part of this route being narrow gauge tramway. This line was converted to electric power in 1929 and this equipment is still in use today, the varnished wooden rolling-stock resplendent with brass trim and the spectacular scenery making it popular with tourists. By contrast, the FCdeM remained faithful to steam until the early 1960s, although by then steam and internal combustion had existed side by side for some time. At all events, the country served by the larger company was less dramatic and, except near Arenal, did not serve any of the areas that were eventually affected by the tourist exploitation of the island, so the railway was ignored by the visitor.

One of the features that attracted me to the FCdeM was the broad range of rolling-stock in use up to the end of steam. The company was established under a strong British influence and the line was equipped with Nasmyth Wilson locomotives and rolling-stock by Brown Marshall of Birmingham — a definite

Goods vehicles belonging to the Soller Railway. The vans on the FCdeM were similar but a couple of feet shorter in length. Some had roof-top screw brake handles with a brakeman's seat let into one end of the body.

A Soller Railway train at Palma. This line has been modelled by Ron Jennings in HOn3 and his layout has been featured in Continental Modeller *magazine.*

feeling of Victorian England transposed to a hot climate. This association lasted until the First World War when Spanish firms were patronized for both locomotives and rolling-stock. Finally, German firms contributed steam locomotives and the modern railcars. This made for a truly cosmopolitan image as many of the earliest steam classes lasted until the end with spindly British 4-4-0 tank locomotives working alongside typically Teutonic designs covered with external plumbing and taking full advantage of the loading gauge.

This mixture makes for added interest when the layout is exhibited, many people thinking it must be 'freelance'. If possible, I try to display some of the older photographs in my collection to prove it actually existed. The final attraction, for me, is that as far as I know nobody else has attempted a model of the FCdeM, although Ron Jennings' HOn3 version of the Soller Railway has appeared in *Continental Modeller* magazine.

Researching the project

Something I did not take fully into consideration at the start of the project was the size and scope of the research which would be needed. As the work progressed, more and more details were necessary; what should the local telegraph poles look like, what colour are Spanish oil drums, what about house designs? These were among the many questions for which I suddenly needed answers. Luckily, although the initial work before construction of a model could begin took about two years, and still continues, the task proved to be a great pleasure, though patience has been needed. The thrill of opening an envelope to find inside the answer to a vital question posed some time earlier, or a photocopy of an out-of-print article on the line (not always in English), became as great as that of seeing a newly-constructed model go through its paces for the first time. Links with several

railway enthusiasts have been formed and I should particularly like to pay tribute to those who have allowed me the freedom of their photographic records. Without their help I doubt whether the model would have been possible. I now have three albums of pictures of the FCdeM, two of them being my own efforts while on holiday in 1981 and later in 1984, while the third forms a historical record of the line covering the period 1955-1974, from just before the end of steam power, through the loss of the goods services to the present passengers-only railcar era.

Bearing in mind the difficulties inherent in undertaking research of a period thirty years ago and in another country, I have adopted the well-proven method of modelling a 'might have been' situation. An extension from the

inland terminus of La Puebla to the nearby ferry port of Alcudia was proposed during the heyday of the line in the early 1930s, but owing to the Spanish Civil War and developing road transport the scheme never materialized. This approach meant that various scattered items from different locations on the FCdeM could be brought together in a fictional setting that would still be true to life without needing total fidelity to the prototype. Thus the station building is a shortened version of La Puebla, which has also provided the water tank and walled storage yard, the toilet building has come from Empalme, while the engine shed is loosely based on one of the sheds at Palma.

As can be appreciated, at least one field trip is an essential part of the research for a project of this nature, and what more could be asked than that it should combine railways and sunny beaches? My first visit in 1981 started with a bicycle trip inland to the town of La Puebla which also included the next two stations along the line, Muro and Llubi. At each location I sketched the general layout, pacing out the dimensions of the loop track and other useful distances. In addition, I recorded full details of the buildings at the terminus with rough drawings to back up the photographs. Unfortunately I was too late to see trains serving the line, as services had been discontinued some three months earlier for 'renovation', a narrow gauge euphemism often meaning total abandonment. Quick measurements in the station yard proved that the repairs were indeed needed, the track gauge being as much as one inch out on either side of

Left *The station building at La Puebla on the FCdeM in 1981. Typical features are the louvred shutters and the bell hanging over the platform. The station name appears on the end wall* (Giles Barnabe).

Right *Who could resist the modelling appeal of structures like this water tank at La Puebla?* (Giles Barnabe).

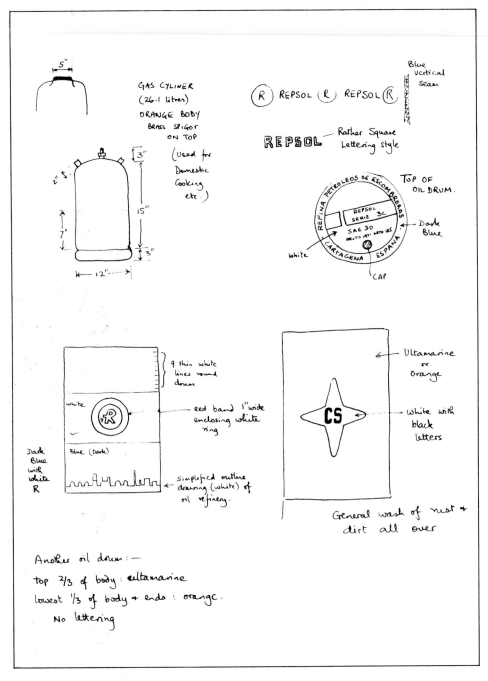

5"

GAS CYLINER
(26.1 litres)
ORANGE BODY
BRASS SPIGOT
ON TOP

(Used for
Domestic
Cooking
etc.)

3"
2"
15"
7"
3"
|← 12" →|

Ⓡ REPSOL Ⓡ REPSOL Ⓡ

Blue
vertical
seam

REPSOL — Rather Square
Lettering style

REFINA PETROLEOS DE ESCOMBRERAS

REPSOL
SERIE 3C
SAE 30
BRUTO 1971 NETO 165

CARTAGENA ESPAÑA

white

TOP OF
OIL DRUM.

Dark
Blue

CAP

9 thin white
lines round
drum

white

Ⓡ

red band 1"wide
enclosing white
ring

Dark
Blue
with
white
R

Blue (Dark)

simplified outline
drawing (white) of
oil refinery.

CS

Ultamarine
or
Orange

white with
black
letters

General wash of rust +
dirt all over

Another oil drum :—

top 2/3 of body : ultamarine
lowest 1/3 of body + ends : orange.
    No lettering

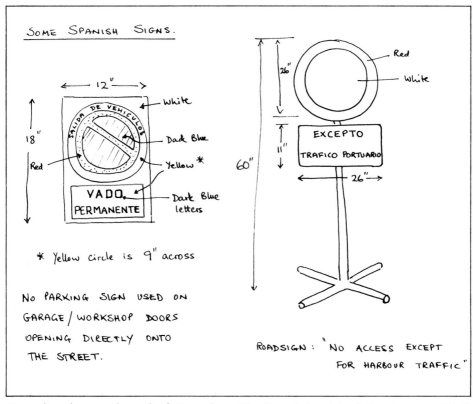

Opposite, above and overleaf *Pages from Giles Barnabe's notebook showing many details important in modelling an overseas prototype realistically.*

the nominal thirty-six inches.

A later trip to Palma found that the railcars were still running on part of the three-foot track, though only as far as the market town of Inca, in the centre of the island. I was unable to ride the train on this occasion, which was a pity as the railcars were using the loop through the locomotive workshops to reach the main line at the station throat, a route normally hidden from public view. All the remaining tracks in the station yard had been torn out and a much simpler layout, laid to metre gauge, was under

construction. I did manage to capture the details of the last survivor of the once numerous F-class brake vans, standing marooned on the site of the old goods yard.

Across the road, beside the FCdeM station, is the neat terminus of the Palma-Soller railway, much smaller than its neighbour and flanked by the backs of tall buildings. One platform, several loops and a carriage shed are ample for today's traffic needs, though formerly there was a tiny goods yard whose access to the running lines was by wagon

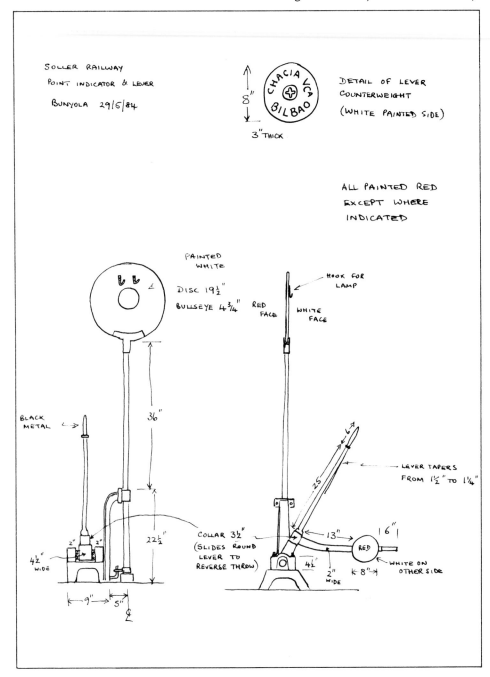

SOLLER RAILWAY
POINT INDICATOR & LEVER
BUNYOLA 29/5/84

8"
3" THICK

CHACIA VCA BILBAO

DETAIL OF LEVER
COUNTERWEIGHT
(WHITE PAINTED SIDE)

ALL PAINTED RED
EXCEPT WHERE
INDICATED

PAINTED
WHITE

DISC 19½"
BULLSEYE 4¾"

RED
FACE

WHITE
FACE

HOOK FOR
LAMP

BLACK
METAL

36"

2"   2"

4½"
WIDE

22½"

COLLAR 3½"
(SLIDES ROUND
LEVER TO
REVERSE THROW)

9"   5"

25"

LEVER TAPERS
FROM 1½" TO 1¼"

13"

6"

RED

4½"

2"
WIDE

8"

WHITE ON
OTHER SIDE

turntable, a typical feature of this railway.

On a subsequent trip to Majorca, visits were again paid to Palma and several runs were made on both lines. By this time the FCdeM gauge conversion had been completed as a single line to Inca while the second track was operational as far as Santa Maria. It is possible that the conversion has been extended beyond Inca since 1984, although, with the exception of Manacor and La Puebla, few towns would seem capable of providing enough traffic to pay for the work involved. The only benefit might be to remove some of the local traffic from the roads during the summer months when they are crowded with tourist coaches.

Much of the second visit was spent tracing the course of the abandoned sections, this time by means of a hired car. Now that VAT has come to Spain, this is a rather costly exercise as hired cars attract 33% tax; luckily, my visit was just within the pre-tax era. However, some means of independent transport is a must to reach some of the railway sites on the island, and they certainly repay the trouble.

On an expedition such as this the opportunity must be taken to record as much detail as possible. One can never have too many pictures, and shots from several angles will not be wasted. If possible, include an article of known size in the composition so that an accurately scaled drawing can be prepared later as an aid to model-making. If this is not possible, make a rough drawing with relevant dimensions added, as a back-up in case of photographic mishaps. Some views across the railway fence, if indeed it even exists, will also be a help to conjure up the scene when it may not be so fresh in the memory.

Certain basic equipment is needed for a field trip, especially one in a hot climate. Firstly get a good map of the area to be covered; in the case of Majorca, Firestone publish a useful map which is obtainable in this country. As well as showing all the railways, including the closed sections, it also indicates which towns have petrol stations — essential information for a motorist where petrol pumps are few and far between. Above all, avoid those tourist maps which will be on sale locally, and which cover the ground with pictures of the 'sights'. What topographical detail they carry may well be suspect in detail. By con-

Recording every detail — a Soller Railway point operating lever and indicator disc. (Giles Barnabe).

trast, the Firestone maps give an indica-
tion of the type of surface and width of
the roads shown. When it says unmetall-
ed surface, it often means rough stony
track suitable only for mules or testing
tanks; it is best to be warned of these
conditions in advance before being
stuck between two dry stone walls with
not enough room to turn round and with
a twelve-inch deep step in front of the
car — I speak from bitter experience!

The only station I had difficulty in finding was the junction at Empalme, which
turned out to be at the end of just such a
country lane as described above, and one
which seemed to be the private road to a
large farm. Eventually I had to walk the
tracks for a mile, to the dismay of some
sheep being driven through a bridge
under the line who had clearly never seen
anything moving on top of the embankment before. Track walking on the
FCdeM is not an easy task as the lumps of
stone used as ballast are rather large and
not well compacted, leading to the risk of
a turned ankle. At the same time, the
sleeper spacing is varied so that a walking
pace is difficult to maintain, and a
somewhat lurching stumble is about the
best that can be achieved.

Apart from a map, a decent camera is a
must, plus whatever accessories your
lensmanship and pocket demand.
Always ensure a good supply of film as
Murphy's Law of Spanish Photography
states that you are most likely to run out
in the middle of an uninhabited
wilderness during the siesta, just as you
discover a new site full of details to
record! Also needed is a sketch-pad,
preferably one with a spiral wire spine,
together with several pencils, the means
to sharpen them, an eraser and a ruler. A
folding three-foot rule may be of more
use than a soft tape measure which may

need a helper to hold the other end.
Despite the small drawback of having to
measure buildings in multiples of one
yard, it has the advantage of being able to
reach above head height for doorways
and other architectural details. Some
years ago I was given a stout leather sat-
chel, bulging with flaps and pockets, and
I find this invaluable for my surveying
gear, picnic lunch, bottled water, hat and
anything else I can cram into it.

To complete the picture obtained
from site visits, a certain amount of book
research is necessary. I soon found a
copy of *Mediterranean Island Railways*
by P.M Kalla-Bishop, which includes a
good history of both lines as well as a
locomotive list. This has been invaluable
in piecing together rough translations of
other articles which I have been sent,
written in French and Catalan. The latter
account included a timetable, working
diagram and drivers' roster for 1973, as
well as a dimensional sketch of the
modern railcars; ample compensation
for the somewhat impenetrable prose.
Do not ignore foreign works of
reference. I recently browsed through a
copy of *La Construccion de Loco-
motoras de Vapor en España* and found
maker's engravings of the Maquinista-
built 2-6-OTs used on the island. These
were rear three-quarter views, the only
information yet found of the bunker end
of these engines. Another Continental
book I am hoping to run to earth is the
out-of-print *Carrilets de España y Por-
tugal — vol 1, España*. This covers many
of the once prolific Spanish narrow
gauge lines, and luckily has an English
translation. In fact, almost any book that
looks as if it might have a Majorcan
reference is now examined. If a solitary
picture is included, a letter is sent to the
photographer via the publisher, enclos-

ing a reply paid envelope. If it is neatly presented, states why the information is required and offers to meet any expenses involved, the result is often the arrival of a set of prints of historical interest, or the name of another contact who may be able to provide the information.

Museums and reference libraries are also a profitable hunting-ground. The Science Museum has records of the Nasmyth engines which can be inspected by appointment, while copies of the maker's photographs were finally run to earth in Salford Public Library, who hold the original prints and can supply copies for sale. Only the most general dimensions of the British-built locomotives have survived, but enough together with the photographs and the known dimensions of other items of rolling-stock to enable models to be constructed that capture the feel of the original, although they might not satisfy a rivet-counter. I must admit to having shied away from such in-depth work on the Spanish and German locomotives, and these models have merely been scaled up from pictures.

The original rolling-stock designs are held by Birmingham Public Library where they form part of the archives of Metro-Cammell, the successors of Brown Marshall & Co. Here at the Local Affairs section of the library one can inspect the catalogues of the archive (including many foreign as well as British railways, both standard and narrow gauge) and also view microfilm of the original Victorian working drawings, which can be ordered in photocopy form; delivery takes about two weeks. These drawings are not copied in their original format and may have been photographed slightly creased, but most include enough decipherable dimensions from which to scale up an accurate copy. Available FCdeM drawings include a van with a roof-top brakeman's seat, two types of open wagon and several four-wheeled carriages.

The models

At the outset, the decision was taken to use a scale of 7mm/ft, despite the discrepancy that would arise with the track gauge where Peco 0-16.5 Crazy Track was to be used. In this way, spare parts and castings for both 4mm and 7mm scale could be used. I did consider the more correct 5.5mm/ft scale but felt that this would cause the locomotive bodies to be too small to fit commercially available mechanisms — I tend to be a model basher rather than a true builder from scratch.

The mechanisms themselves come from almost as many sources as did the prototype locomotives: the Nasmyth 4-4-OT has an old Triang Midland '2P' mechanism, while a Hornby Ivatt with slightly modified valve gear was used to power the Spanish 2-6-OT. A Fleischmann Black Anna was used for the Nasmyth 0-4-OT while Piko provided the works for the two internal combustion vehicles, an early railcar and a works railmotor. Bodywork is styrene sheet with Plastruct tubing for the boilers. Commercial castings for boiler mountings were modified to resemble the prototype's fittings, and all the motive power was built from photographs as I was unable to obtain full dimensional details.

Hornby wagon underframes were used, though much modified. The brakegear was first removed with a sharp craft knife and the axleguards' facing detail was removed and if necessary their shape altered so that white metal castings could be glued on top to back-date their appearance. Some of the prototype axle-guards had very wide 'W' irons with long springs, which were made up from scraps of styrene where commercially available castings were unsuitable. New brake levers were provided from styrene or 7mm scale white metal wagon parts, as were brake blocks made from lumps of balsa wood glued to flat wire hangers made from flattened office staples. Some of the vans have roof-top brake standards which were soldered up from scrap wire and lend an exotic touch to goods trains. Because the new wagon bodies are so much wider than their chassis, new solebars were provided either in styrene or else using Plastruct channel sections. Wood graining was simulated by dragging a fine-toothed saw blade along the wagon body after the gaps between the planks had been scribed. Originally it was hoped to use Fleischmann couplings as these almost resembled the chopper couplers of the

prototype. However, a combination of long wheelbase wagons and sharp curves led to the adoption of Hornby couplings as standard. Wagon livery was something of a problem as all my older picture references were monochrome. However, I have recently been sent some colour slides that confirm that almost all the rolling-stock was painted a reddish-brown colour (rather more brown than red in the case of the carriages). Most of the wagons and some of the coaches had been weathered down to almost bare timber which probably accounts for the description in one magazine of 'lines of grey wagons'. Where possible, wagons have been numbered from actual known examples.

Setting the scene

One of the challenges of modelling a foreign prototype is capturing the local atmosphere correctly. It has to be distilled and presented to a viewer who is probably more used to the modelling con-

The Nasmyth Wilson 4-4-0T based on a Hornby 'L1' chassis heads a passenger train at Alcudia. The Gakken coaches are not unlike the original Brown Marshall-built carriages (Len Weal).

The Spanish-built 2-6-0T modelled on a Hornby Ivatt chassis leaves Alcudia with a goods train (Len Weal).

ventions of a British landscape in such a way that the location of the layout is immediately apparent. Working in 7mm scale on a limited baseboard area (actually two pasting tables) means that most structures have to be fairly small, the more so as the two main baseboards each fold in half for transport. The waterfront buildings needed particularly careful placing and the heights of the roofs were calculated to a fraction of an inch. Luckily, the traditional architectural style is a simple one with no frills, and, as the layout is set in the pre-concrete era, nothing is taller than a couple of storeys. The buildings are either made of stone blocks or rendered with cement or plaster; the former is simulated by applying white glue to the card structure and then gently rolling on damp Pyruma. Before this sets, the lines

between the stone blocks can be scored. A quicker treatment is the rendering, done either with diluted Pyruma or DIY plaster filler applied straight from the pot with a half-inch wide flat brush. With care, lintels can be built up with this method, but otherwise card overlays are provided to build up the extra thickness involved. The roofs feature Wills pantiles; where these sheets are too small in themselves, they are butted together and any thin cracks filled with Milliput, which is also used for the roof ridge-tiles. Almost all the windows are covered with louvred shutters, mostly modified from some I had at hand. Sheds and non-dwelling structures have plank shutters which are easier to construct. A subtle touch on the more recently-built models is the signwriting in Spanish style; the letters are rather square with few diagonal

A general view of Giles Barnabe's 'Alcudia' 7mm scale 16.5mm gauge layout showing the typical Spanish-style structures (Len Weal).

lines. Hopefully the combination of peeling walls, pantiles and shutters will set the scene for anyone who has enjoyed a Mediterranean holiday.

To help give the impression of heat, the colours used in the scenery are much paler than those commonly used on British layouts. Although non-specific, the period portrayed is probably late spring before the heat of summer bleaches everything to a pale straw colour. Shades varying from pale fawn to deep cream were blended for the basic earth colour which was painted all over the landscape. Dust and crushed Majorcan rock was sifted over the paint while it was still wet and light green and yellow foliage by Woodland Scenics was used for weeds. What the layout then needed was some trees, as on the prototype the station platforms always enjoyed natural shade rather than glass awnings. Most models including the rolling-stock, were weathered with pale earth shades or

even off-white to provide a dry, dusty atmosphere.

Small details are also important to set the scene. Telephone poles are kebab sticks with white-metal insulators adapted from commercial white-metal castings. These are rather fragile and a stronger version can easily be made from the thinnest single-core bell-wire. Tamiya produce oil drums for wargamers and these, though slightly overscale, can be quite useful. The local design is either painted orange or sea green with three large four-pointed stars around the centre and carrying the initials CS. Another firm is Repsol with a blue-white-blue colour scheme with an R-in-a-circle logo and the name repeated round the central panel. CEPSA drums are pale grey with orange or red stripes and lettering which would be rather difficult to achieve on a round object in such a small scale.

One of my reference photographs

The station pilot, a Nasmyth Wilson-built 0-4-0T shunts a van on to the factory siding at Alcudia, with the locomotive shed to the left of the picture (Giles Barnabe).

shows an old lorry rotting away inside the Palma roundhouse in the 1960s, when it must have been at least forty years old, and a Yesteryear 'Lowenbrau' lorry has been rebuilt to resemble it. Local commercial vehicles over an approximately one-ton rating carry at the rear a blue plate some nine inches square with a thin yellow border. This indicates the name of the town of registration, the initials PM in the case of Palma. This touch is another of the little details that anyone who has visited the island will remember, and which will help the look of 'foreignness' to an uninitiated viewer.

Much of the agricultural produce of the era being modelled would have

Nasmyth Wilson 4-4-0T Salinas arriving at Alcudia with a goods train. The locomotive features a Hornby 2P mechanism, motion modified from Hornby 'King Arthur' parts with styrene bodywork built around a Compound body. The wagons have scratchbuilt styrene bodies on Hornby wagon underframes (Giles Barnabe).

been brought to the railhead in two-wheeled farm carts, but I need to find some model mules or rather bony horses before tackling this scene. Road signs can be photocopied from Highway Code publications or drawn oversize and reduced on a photo-copier. The 'No Parking' sign seen on all doorways used by vehicles has been tackled in this way and coloured with felt-tipped pens. Another scene to in-clude is an outdoor café with some tables and chairs competing for space with drying fishing-nets, fish boxes and, of course, the trains that pick their way through the chaos of the quayside.

The local population of Alcudia is, by a quirk of fate, being represented by Spanish 7mm scale figures bought many years ago when I was in the clockwork-on-the-carpet phase of rail-ways. Amazingly they have survived, and include a Civil Guard with his black leather hat and a peasant with a cloth bundle and a fowl in a basket as his luggage. All that was needed was to remove the large cast bases from the figures and repaint them in matt col-ours. They have been supplemented by a man, presumably one of the rare tourists to discover the FCdeM, who is lurking at the end of the platform with his Box Brownie camera, and a Slater's Guard. The latter has had his overcoat shortened to jacket length and his flag removed to become the 'Jefe de Esta-cion' about to ring the station bell to signal the train's departure.

I wish I had thought to photograph the real railway staff's uniforms while I had the chance. From memory, the present dress is a medium to dark blue lightweight jacket (worn somewhat loose) with perhaps slightly darker trousers. Caps vary considerably be-tween countries and the present Spanish design has a rather low crown and not much overhang at the sides; the peak is fairly small. Details just discernable in some of the pictures sug-gest that twenty years ago the tops of the caps were larger, and the style of uniform was slightly more formally cut in a heavier material. Footplate staff ap-pear in the usual boiler suits or bib-and-braces overalls. Headgear is invariably a beret rather than a grease-top cap.

In conclusion

Many of the remarks concerning research would be equally applicable to a modeller setting out to portray one of the more esoteric British railways. The moral is: if you see a picture that in-spires a model, do not be put off if the information seems a little scarce at first. With patience you will succeed, and the result is quite likely to be a unique model.

Index